BIOLOGY
PROJECTS
FOR YOUNG
SCIENTISTS

BIOLOGY PROJECTS FOR YOUNG SCIENTISTS

Salvatore Tocci

FRANKLIN WATTS
A Division of Grolier Publishing
New York ▪ London ▪ Hong Kong ▪ Sydney
Danbury, Connecticut

NOTE TO READERS:

Throughout this book, most measurements are given only in metric units because that is the system of measure used by most professional scientists. Words in *italics* appear in the Glossary at the back of this book.

Photographs ©: Peter Arnold Inc.: 75 (Roland Birke), 95 (Leonard Lessing), cover (Alfred Pasieka), 54 (Ed Reschke), 98 (SIU); Photo Researchers: 44 (Bio-photo Assoc.), 114 (Oliver Meckes), 92 (OMIKRON), 71 (Rod Planck), 126 (Andrew Syred/SPL); Tom Pantages: 27; Tony Stone Images: 36 (Wayne Eastep); Visuals Unlimited: 22 (Mike Abbey), 78 (Cabisco), 108 (J. D. Cunningham), 25, 68 (Stanley L. Flegler), 39 (Science VU/Sidney Fox), 60, 99 (David M. Phillips), 76 (L. S. Stepanowicz).

Visit Franklin Watts on the Internet at:
http://publishing.grolier.com

Library of Congress Cataloging-in-Publication Data

Tocci, Salvatore
    Biology projects for young scientists/Salvatore Tocci—Rev. Ed.
    p.   cm. — (Projects for young scientists)
Includes bibliographical references and index.
Summary: A collection of biological science projects that demonstrate concepts and aspects of photosynthesis, genetics, plant and animal development, cell structure, and biochemistry.
ISBN 0-531-11703-1 (lib. bdg.)   0-531-16460-8 (pbk.)
1. Biology projects.—Juvenile literature.   2. Biology—Experiments.
[1. Biology—Experiments.   2. Experiments.]   I. Title.   II. Series
QH316.5.T63   1999
570'.78—dc21   98-46560
                                                                      CIP
                                                                      AC

CONTENTS

BIOLOGY
PROJECTS
FOR YOUNG
SCIENTISTS

CHAPTER 1

GETTING STARTED

You are probably reading this book because you are looking for an idea for a biology project. Maybe you are completing a class assignment. Or maybe your school is sponsoring a science fair, and you want to enter it. It is also possible that you want to do a project to earn some extra credit. And there is always the chance that you are looking for project ideas just because you are interested in learning more about biology. No matter what the reason, you have come to the right place.

This book contains biology projects that can be done either in school or at home. To help you get started, each project begins with some background information. A section called "What You Need" lists the materials and equipment you will need to complete the project. This book does not provide instructions about how to use specific types of equipment or how to prepare solutions. If you need help, check a science reference book or ask your science teacher for guidance.

If you would like to expand a project and want a greater challenge, look at the "Doing More" sections that follows each project. Most of these suggestions will require additional research—both for more detailed information about the topic and for techniques required to carry out the project. Some of the resources listed in the Appendix may help you. If not, ask your science teacher or a librarian for help, or search for information on the Internet. Be sure that you plan and carry out your work under the supervision of your science teacher or an adult. Some of these projects involve the use of poisonous chemicals, boiling solutions, or sophisticated procedures.

DECIDING WHAT TO DO

You have probably chosen to do a biology project because you enjoyed learning about life sciences in school. When you read your textbooks, you probably thought scientists know all about living things and can explain how every organism functions. After all, most textbooks describe what scientists have discovered and explain how biological principles operate in nature or in the laboratory. But do not be fooled! There are still many things that scientists do not know. Many areas need to be explored and countless questions need to be answered. In fact, all scientists could write more about what they do not know than what they do know. Just think, your biology project may add something new to what scientists know about the world around us.

Even though you plan to undertake a project in biology, you probably don't know how to get started. Don't be dismayed. The hardest part of any science project is deciding exactly what you want to do. Start by making a list of your interests and hobbies. For example, if you like gardening, then you may want to do a biology project that involves plants. If you found *heredity* interesting when you studied it in biology class, then you may want to carry out a project in *genetics*. If you love animals, try a project that investigates some aspect of their development. If you really have no idea of what you want to do, this book can help. It contains information for projects in all areas of biology.

Most of the projects in this book focus on animals. As you will discover in Chapter 3, biology includes a wide variety of living things. Besides animals, there are plants, fungi, and a variety of microorganisms. Although the book has a few projects involving plants, if you are most interested in doing a project with plants, you may want to read a book called *Botany Projects for Young Scientists*.

OBTAINING INFORMATION ABOUT YOUR PROJECT

Once you have chosen a subject, you should read as much as possible about it. All good scientists read everything they can about their field. Reading will provide you with important background information and help you narrow your topic to a specific question or problem.

Begin your research in the school library. Read a few books on your topic, then look for articles in science magazines and professional journals. These periodicals will have the most up-to-date information. If your school doesn't have all the resources you need, check with a librarian at a local college. Because articles in professional journals are written by scientists and are intended for other scientists, many of them will be too technical for you to understand. If you come across an article that seems relevant to your topic, ask your science teacher to help you understand it.

Be sure to check the multimedia encyclopedias that are available through on-line computer services such as America Online and Microsoft Network. These services also provide access to the Internet, an extremely valuable resource for obtaining information to help you with your biology project. In effect, the Internet is the world's largest "information mall." You can "shop," or search, for anything, including ideas for your biology project.

The part of the Internet that many people find most useful in searching for information is the World Wide Web. Searching, or "surfing," the Web can be somewhat intimidating at first. Using a directory, which consists of hundreds of thousands of documents sorted into various categories, can make your search much easier. Among the most popular directories are Yahoo (*http://www.yahoo. com/*) and Magellan (*http://magellan.excite.com/*).

For a more focused search, you can use an index with the help of a tool known as a search engine. Several search engines and their Web addresses are listed in Table 1. To use an index, all you do is type in one or more keywords. The more specific your keywords are, the more focused your search will be. For example, if your keyword is "plants," you will probably get millions of hits. Each hit represents a Web page that contains information about the keyword(s) you entered. Obviously, you could spend more time going through these Web pages than you will on the project itself. But if you type in the keywords "plants + nutrients + growth," the list of documents that comes up will be much shorter and will focus on the topic of nutrients needed for plant growth.

TABLE 1: Accessing an Index on the Web

Search Engine	Address
Alta Vista	*http://altavista.com*
Excite	*http://www.excite.com/*
Inktomi HotBot	*http://www.hotbot.com/*
Infoseek	*http://infoseek.go.com/*
Lycos	*http://lycos.cs.cmu.edu/*
Open Text	*http://www.opentext.com/*
Webcrawler	*http://webcrawler.com*

By the way, each search engine uses its own search techniques. Some require you to put quotation marks around the words to show that they go together. Others require you to type "and" or the sign "+" between words to show you're looking for sites that contain all the keywords and not just one of them. Check the search engine's instructions for the most efficient way to conduct a search.

If you enjoy working with computers, you could use a computer as part of your project in other ways. For example, you may want to develop a program to simulate a real-life situation. You may find it difficult, if not impossible, to conduct a project investigating the pattern of evolution in some large organism. But with a computer, you might be able to create a simulation that mimics the real world and predict what might happen. As you read this book, keep computer capabilities in mind. You might be able to use software programs to add a new dimension to your project.

SCIENTIFIC PROCESSES

Once you feel knowledgeable about your topic, begin to plan your project. Most people think scientists always follow a set routine, called the scientific method, when they work. The scientific method is usually described as a set of steps—collecting information, forming a hypothesis, carrying out an experiment, and drawing a conclusion. In reality, the scientific method is not a set routine, and scientists do not depend solely on one method in their work. They rely upon a wide variety of methods known as scientific processes. See Table 2.

TABLE 2: Scientific Processes	
Step	**Methods for Accomplishing Step**
Collecting information	Observing, conducting field studies, measuring, sampling
Hypothesizing	Forming a hypothesis, predicting
Experimenting	Conducting a controlled experiment, problem solving, analyzing data, evaluating data, communicating
Drawing conclusions	Modeling, inferring, forming a theory

An accurate definition of the term "scientific method" includes a variety of scientific processes that are used to answer a specific question. For example, if a group of scientists wants to determine whether a drug can be used to treat a particular disease, their scientific method would most likely involve forming a hypothesis, carrying out a controlled experiment, evaluating the data, drawing a conclusion, and communicating the findings. However, the scientific method used by scientists studying the evolution of birds might include collecting and analyzing data in the field, examining museum collections, sharing findings with other scientists, and forming a hypothesis. Whatever scientific processes you decide to use will be the scientific method for your biology project.

If one of the processes you decide to use involves an experiment, be careful to include a *control group* whenever necessary. A control group serves as a standard of comparison. Scientists carrying out an experiment often set up two groups that are identical in all respects but one. One group—the *experimental group*—is subjected to the factor being investigated; the other—the control group—is not.

For example, if you wish to test the effect of radiation on the growth of earthworms, you would expose the worms in the experimental group to X rays. You would keep the worms in the control group in identical physical surroundings and feed them the same food, but you would not expose them to any radiation. If radiation affects earthworms, you should observe a noticeable difference between the worms in the experimental group and those in the control group.

Experiments also involve variables—something that changes. In the preceding example, the X rays are the *independent variable*—the factor you can change any way you wish. For example, you can decide the quantity of radiation used, the length of time the radiation is given, the number of exposures administered, and so on. The growth of the earthworms is known as the *dependent variable*. It changes based on what you do with the independent variable. For example, you may find that when more radiation is given (the independent variable), the growth of the earthworms (the dependent variable) is more severely retarded.

BE THOROUGH AND LOOK FOR THE UNEXPECTED

No matter what scientific processes you use, be sure to neatly record your observations and data in a notebook that is used only for your project. Your notebook might include written descriptions, numerical data, drawings, or photographs. Make graphs and tables to organize your numerical data. A computer spreadsheet program may be helpful.

Record everything you observe—even if it doesn't seem important. Close observation may reveal something that is totally unexpected. As you may know, Alexander Fleming accidentally discovered penicillin in the 1920s. He noticed that no bacteria grew near mold that had formed on some of his dirty culture dishes. Fleming reasoned that the mold must be secreting a substance that killed the bacteria. The substance turned out to be penicillin—the first of many antibiotics that have saved millions of lives.

Penicillin is only one of the many important accidental discoveries made by alert scientists. In the 1960s, Barnett Rosenberg made an observation similar to Fleming's. Rosenberg noticed that bacteria failed to grow near metal probes he was using to generate electric fields.

SAFETY FIRST

All projects should be done under the supervision of a parent, a teacher, or a professional scientist. The more complicated the project, the more you will need to know about proper procedures and safety precautions. Be sure to discuss safety with the person supervising you. If you have any questions, don't hesitate to ask someone who is knowledgeable about your topic.

No matter what type of project you undertake, always follow safety guidelines. In most cases, this simply means using common sense and keeping a few basic rules in mind.

- Do not eat or drink anything in the laboratory or area where you are carrying out your project.

- Do not taste any chemicals.

- Keep your work area as clean and organized as possible.

- Wear protective eye goggles when working with chemicals.

- Handle toxic or flammable substances with care.

- Read instructions carefully before using any specialized equipment.

- Report any dangerous situations or injuries to the adult supervising you.

- Handle live animals—especially fish, amphibians, reptiles, birds, and mammals—in a thoughtful and humane manner.

- Learn how to properly care for any animal you use in your project.

Eventually, Rosenberg and his coworkers isolated a substance that formed near these probes. The substance, called cisplatin, affected the growth of cells. In 1979, the United States Food and Drug Administration approved the substance as a drug for treating certain types of cancer. Accidental discoveries, such as those made by Fleming and Rosenberg, prove that there is no one scientific method that will lead to an answer, a solution, or a discovery.

SCIENCE COMPETITIONS

You may decide to enter your biology project in a science competition. This is an ideal opportunity to show off your project and have it judged by professionals, perhaps even a scientist whose interests parallel yours. Science fairs are often sponsored by schools and local organizations. Each science fair has its own rules and specifications, so read the entry form and application carefully before planning your project.

Winning projects selected in local competitions are usually entered in regional, state, or even national competitions. The last step would be the International Science and Engineering Fair or the Intel Science Talent Search. To find out about either of these competitions, contact Science Service Inc. at 1719 N Street NW, Washington, DC 20036-2890 or *http://www.sciserv.org*. If your biology project gets you all the way to one of these prestigious competitions, remember that this book may have been the first step to your success.

CHAPTER 2

CHEMICALS IN LIVING THINGS

To understand how living things function, you must first know something about the chemicals present in all organisms. Everything an organism does requires chemicals that react with one another. Many scientists study these chemical reactions. Their task is not a simple one. After all, a single bacterial cell contains more than 5,000 different chemicals. A single human cell has more than 10,000!

In this chapter, you will learn about a few of these chemicals—those that play a major role in biological processes. These chemicals vary widely in size and structure. Some are very small, with simple structures. Others are much larger and have complex structures that twist and fold.

WATER

Water is one of the most important chemicals in your body. Without it, you would die. Water is important for other living things too. In fact, water is the most abundant chemical in all living things. In animals, it is required for digestion, circulation, and most other biological processes. Water accounts for more than 50 percent of your body mass and 90 percent of the fluid part of your blood.

As important as water is for survival, it is possible for an organism to have too much water in its cells. All organisms must have just the right amount of water to survive. Excess water can cause cells to swell, burst, and die. To prevent this from happening, organisms must get rid of extra water.

The most important mechanism organisms use to obtain and eliminate water is called *diffusion*. Diffusion is the process by which a substance, such as water, moves from a region of higher concentration to an area of lower concentration. Before entering or leaving an organism, water must diffuse through the membrane surrounding each cell. This type of diffusion is called *osmosis*. Osmosis maintains an equal concentration of water on both sides of the cellular membrane.

This system works well for animals that live on land, but it could be a potential problem for aquatic organisms. Consider the situation faced by a unicellular (one-celled) organism that lives in freshwater. The concentration of water is higher in its environment than inside its body. Consequently, water continually diffuses into the organism. If the organism did not have any way to eliminate the water, it would swell and eventually burst. Fortunately, aquatic unicellular organisms have a special structure called a *contractile vacuole*. It collects water from various parts of the cell and pumps it out.

MEASURING CONTRACTILE VACUOLE ACTIVITY

For a freshwater unicellular organism to survive, water must be removed from the cell at the same rate it enters. The process of maintaining a constant internal water concentration is called *osmoregulation*. The following project will examine the role contractile vacuoles play in osmoregulation in *Paramecia*.

What You Need	
Toothpick	Coverslip
Glass microscope slide	Microscope
Petroleum jelly	Digital watch or watch with second hand
Paramecium culture	

Using a toothpick, smear a glass microscope slide with a very thin layer of petroleum jelly. Place a small drop of *Paramecium* culture on the petroleum jelly. Add a coverslip. Locate a *Paramecium* that has been trapped between the petroleum jelly and the coverslip. Place the slide under a microscope, and look for the contractile vacuole at one end of the *Paramecium*. Watch as the vacuole fills with water and then suddenly disappears as it bursts to expel the water out into the environment. You will need patience to observe this happening.

Keep track of the time intervals between contractions in a notebook. Do this for a period of 2 to 3 minutes. Repeat this process for the contractile vacuole at the opposite end of the *Paramecium*. Are the rates of water expulsion the same for the two contractile vacuoles? Record the rates of water expulsion for four different

Some unicellular organisms, such as the *Paramecium*, contain two contractile vacuoles. In this photograph, one of the contractile vacuoles has just burst.

Paramecia. How do these rates compare? Why is it a good idea to check the activity of the contractile vacuoles in more than one *Paramecium*?

Doing More

- Determine how contractile vacuoles respond to changes in water concentration in a *Paramecium*'s environment. To alter the water concentration, you can use sucrose—a type of sugar. A chemistry teacher can show you how to prepare a 0.050 molar (M) sucrose solution. Next, mix 1 milliliter (mL) of the *Paramecium* culture with 1 mL of the sucrose solution. This mixture will expose the organism to an environment that is 0.025 M sucrose. Record the rate at which the contractile vacuoles expel water under these conditions. Be sure to observe at least four different *Paramecia*.

  Test different water concentrations by varying the amount of 0.050 M sucrose solution that you add to the *Paramecium* culture. For example, to expose the organisms to a higher sucrose concentration (and thus a lower water concentration), mix 1 mL of *Paramecium* culture with 4 mL of 0.050 M sucrose. The result will be a 0.040 M sucrose environment.

Calculate the rate of water expulsion for each sucrose concentration that you test. The shape of the contractile vacuole is nearly spherical. Thus, its volume can be represented by the formula for the volume of a sphere.

$$v = \frac{d^3 \pi}{6}$$

You can use 3.14 for the value of π. The diameter (*d*) of a contractile vacuole that is filled with water is about 7 micrometers (μm). For each sucrose concentration, calculate the volume (v) of water expelled by the *Paramecia* each minute. Remember that the organisms contain two contractile vacuoles. The volume of water expelled will be expressed in cubic micrometers (μm^3), and the rate of water expulsion will be expressed in cubic micrometers per minute (μm^3/min).

- Investigate the effects of different salt concentrations on the rate at which the contractile vacuoles expel water. Do the effects vary depending on the type of salt used? Try sodium chloride, potassium sulfate, calcium carbonate, and magnesium acetate. What happens if you place the *Paramecia* in distilled water. You can explore other types of environmental changes by varying the temperature, acidity level, and light intensity.

- The pumping mechanism of a contractile vacuole requires energy. This energy is supplied by a chemical called *adenosine triphosphate* (ATP). Certain chemicals, such as 2,4-dinitrophenol, can inhibit the amount of ATP produced by an organism. Plan a project to investigate the relationship between an ATP inhibitor and the action of contractile vacuoles. Attempt to identify a substance that accelerates the pumping action of contractile vacuoles. Design an experiment to test whether that substance speeds up their action by inducing ATP production.

- Unicellular organisms living in saltwater face a different challenge. The concentration of water in their bodies is higher than the concentration of water in their environment. As a result, these organisms tend to lose water. Like their freshwater relatives, these creatures have a special way of maintaining the proper balance of water. For example, diatoms are surrounded by brightly colored shells. These shells help prevent water loss. When diatoms die, their shells pile up. Even though these creatures are microscopic, when large numbers of shells accumulate over time, they can form massive structures, such as the white cliffs of Dover in England.

  Diatom deposits are mined in Kansas, Oregon, Washington, and Nevada. If you live near one of these mines, contact the mining company and ask for permission to photograph one of the shells. You can also find diatoms in the diatomaceous earth sold by pet stores. It is used to filter the water in aquariums.

  The shapes and colors of diatom shells depend on what they are made of. You may want to analyze various shell types to find out what they are made of. Use the Internet to search for references on how to identify silicon, calcium carbonate, and proteins. These are a few of the materials usually found in diatom shells.

This photograph of a diatom was
taken through a microscope. It shows
the diatom magnified more than 4,500 times.

OSMOREGULATION
IN LARGER ORGANISMS

Regulating the internal concentration of water is also a
problem for larger organisms, especially those living in
estuaries or salt marshes. In these areas, the concentrations of water and salt are constantly changing. They are
affected by tides, water currents, rainfall, and land ero-
sion. Animals living in estuaries and salt marshes must be
able to regulate their internal water concentration despite
wide environmental fluctuations.

Obtain some creatures, such as snails or crabs, that
live in an estuary or a salt marsh. If you live close to one

What You Need	
Organisms that live in an estuary or a salt marsh	Plastic tubing
	Air stone
Balance	Distilled water
Fish tank	Salt water
Air pump	Salinometer

of these areas, be sure to check local regulations governing the collection of such creatures. If you live far from an estuary or a salt marsh, you can ask your science teacher to help you order the organisms you need from a science supply company.

Weigh each organism, and invent a system for marking or labeling each one so you can track its progress. During the experiment, you will use changes in body weight to measure water retention. Place the organisms in a fish tank that has been set up to mimic the environment in which the organisms normally live. You may find it necessary to use an air pump, tubing, and an air stone to aerate the water. This will prevent the tank from becoming contaminated with unwanted organisms.

Keep the estuary or salt marsh creatures in the tank for at least 1 week, so they can get acclimated to their new environment. At various times during the week, check the weight of each organism. Because you are not altering the environment, the body weight of each creature should not vary too much. You will be able to see how much weight fluctuates naturally.

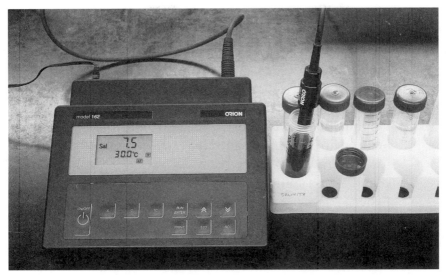

A salinometer

To test the organisms' ability to osmoregulate, replace the water in the tank with water that has a different salt concentration. After a week has passed, record the weight of each organism. You may want to use a computer database program to keep track of your results. Repeat this process several more times with different concentrations of salt solutions. To create various salt solutions, add distilled water to decrease salinity and boil off water to increase salinity. You can use a salinometer to determine the salinity of the salt solutions you make.

By comparing your results at various salinity levels, you will get an idea of how well each organism osmoregulates. In this experiment, what assumption are you making about any weight gain? Weight loss? Use a computer spreadsheet program to calculate the percent change in the weight of each organism over the course of your project.

Doing More

Compare several different types of organisms to see which one best controls its internal water concentration. Conduct your study at different times of the year to see whether the organisms osmoregulate better during a particular season.

- Compare organisms of the same type living in different environments: a saltwater crab versus a brackish-water crab or a saltwater snail versus a freshwater snail. Use a computer program to generate a graph of your results.

- If you discover an organism that is a poor osmoregulator, design a project aimed at improving its capability. Experiment with chemical additives. Diuretics are drugs given to people who have trouble eliminating water in their urine. Other drugs cause people to retain water. Check with your doctor or pharmacist for some specific drugs you can test.

ORGANIC COMPOUNDS

Your body also contains many *organic compounds*—molecules that contain carbon and a combination of other elements, such as hydrogen, oxygen, and nitrogen. Sugars, fats, and proteins are all organic compounds.

Sugars often join together to form larger compounds called starches. Both sugars and starches belong to a group of organic compounds known as *carbohydrates*. Carbohydrates are the principal source of energy for most living things. The energy content of any food substance is measured in calories. One calorie is the amount of energy required to raise 1 gram (g) of water 1 degree Celsius (°C). A device called a calorimeter can be used to measure the energy content of different foods.

BUILDING A CALORIMETER

What You Need	
Protective eye goggles	Small graduated cylinder
Empty coffee can	Water
Metal shears	Metric rule
Large nail	Thermometer
Hammer	Peanut
Large glass test tube	Matches
Small cork	
Pin	

Caution: Wear protective eye goggles while performing this project. You may wany to carry out the following procedure under the supervision of an adult. If so, be sure the adult also wears eye goggles.

Using the metal shears, remove a pie-shaped piece from the side of the coffee can. Invert the can so that the open end is facing down. Using the hammer and nail, carefully make a hole wide enough to hold a large test tube in the bottom of the can. Puncture several more holes around this opening. See Figure 1 on page 30.

Insert a pin into a small cork and place the cork under the can. Using the small graduated cylinder, pour 10 mL of water into the test tube and position it so that the bottom is approximately 2 centimeters (cm) above the pin. After recording the temperature of the water ($T_{initial}$), remove the cork and pin from under the can. Leave the thermometer in the water, and be sure not to move the test tube.

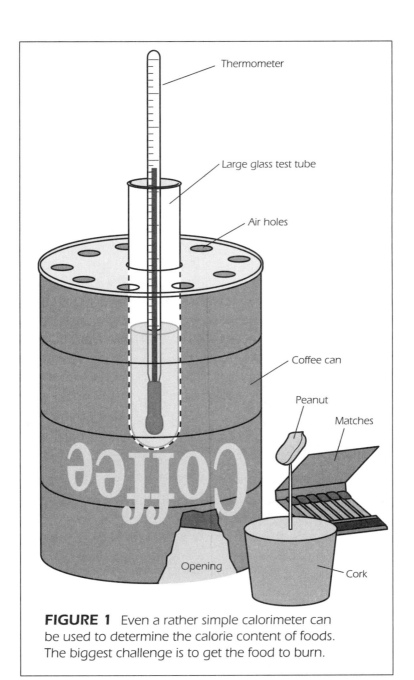

FIGURE 1 Even a rather simple calorimeter can be used to determine the calorie content of foods. The biggest challenge is to get the food to burn.

Insert the pin into the peanut. Ignite the peanut with a match. Once the peanut is burning, carefully place it under the test tube in the calorimeter. After the peanut has completely burned, observe the thermometer to record the highest temperature of the water (T_{final}). Use the following formula to calculate the number of calories in the peanut.

$$\text{calories} = 10 \text{ mL (volume of water)} \times (T_{final} - T_{initial})$$

Are you surprised by the rather large number of calories present in a small peanut? Actually, there are two kinds of calories—the scientific ones and the dietetic ones. In calculating the calorie content of a peanut, you were working with scientific calories, spelled with a small letter. Nutritionists and doctors use the term Calorie. One Calorie equals 1,000 calories. How many Calories did your peanut contain?

Doing More

- Fats contain more energy per gram than any other food. Carbohydrates and proteins contain 4 Calories per gram; fats contain about 9 Calories per gram. Fats belong to a group of organic compounds known as *lipids*. Use your calorimeter to determine the calorie content of a lipid, such as piece of cured pork fat or lard. Use a balance to be sure the fat sample has the same mass as that of a peanut. If you have difficulty igniting the fat sample, use a small piece of string as a wick. Mold the fat around the string, and then ignite the string. You may have to repeat this process several times before you are successful in igniting the fat.

- Not all the heat energy released by the burning food sample is transferred to the water. To determine the calorie content of foods with greater accuracy, scientists use insulated calorimeters. Ask your science teacher to help you. Construct such a calorimeter. Repeat your procedure and compare the results to those obtained with your original calorimeter.

- Calories not used by the body are converted into fat tissue. Recent guidelines issued by the U.S. government indicate that more than half of American adults are overweight. Design a computer program that allows the user to enter the foods eaten on a given day (calorie input), the types of exercise done on that day (calories used), and the grams of fat that result from any remaining calories. Be sure your program takes the person's gender, age, and other physical characteristics into consideration.

PROTEINS

Most of the organic compounds in animals are *proteins*. Proteins are made from chemical building blocks called *amino acids*. There are many different types of proteins involved in biological processes. Proteins can be classified into two major groups. One group includes proteins that contribute to the structure of an organism. For example, the skin and muscles of animals are made mostly of proteins.

The second group of proteins includes *enzymes*. An enzyme is a chemical substance that increases the rate of a chemical reaction. Most enzymes are proteins. A lack of any of the body's enzymes can have serious consequences. Without the enzyme, an organism may be unable to function normally and may even die. In the following project, you will have the chance to explore some properties of enzymes. In fact, you can learn a great deal about enzymes by working with just a few chemicals and something you probably love to eat—liver.

ASSAYING ENZYME ACTIVITY

What You Need	
3% hydrogen peroxide	Bunsen burner or hot plate
Test tubes	Matches
Liver	Sand
Graduated cylinder	Pencil
Freezer	
Beaker	

Liver contains an enzyme called catalase. This enzyme speeds up the breakdown of hydrogen peroxide, a poisonous chemical continually produced by organisms. In the presence of catalase, hydrogen peroxide is quickly broken down into two harmless substances—water and oxygen.

Carefully pour 5 mL of 3% hydrogen peroxide into a test tube. *Caution: Hydrogen peroxide is poisonous, and it can irritate your skin and eyes. Be sure to wear gloves, safety goggles, and an apron or a smock.* Add a piece of liver about the size of a pea and observe what happens. After the reaction stops, divide the contents into two test tubes. Add another piece of liver to one test tube and 5 mL of fresh hydrogen peroxide to the other. Did the liver, hydrogen peroxide, or both remain unchanged after the first reaction? You can vary the amounts of liver and hydrogen peroxide to see what concentrations work best.

Test the effects of temperature on enzyme action. Try freezing the liver overnight and then test its effectiveness after thawing. Next, try boiling the liver in water for 10 minutes before adding it to the hydrogen peroxide. Which liver sample produced more gas bubbles?

To test the effect of changing the surface area on the rate of enzyme activity, place a pea-sized piece of liver in a clean test tube. Crush the liver by adding a small amount of sand and grinding the mixture with the eraser end of a pencil. Add 5 mL of fresh hydroxide peroxide to the crushed liver. Observe what happens. Compare the results to what happened when you added hydrogen peroxide to uncrushed liver. Crushing the liver greatly increases its surface area and exposes many more enzymes to the hydrogen peroxide.

Doing More

- For a more precise way of testing the relationship between enzyme concentration and the rate of the reaction, try using your saliva. Saliva contains an enzyme capable of breaking down starch.

  Chew a piece of gum to stimulate the release of saliva. Collect 5 mL of your saliva in a test tube. Dilute the saliva with distilled water to prepare different concentrations. For example, mix 1 mL of saliva with 9 mL of water to dilute it 10 times. Add 1 mL of this diluted solution to 9 mL of water to make a sample that is 100 times more dilute than the original saliva.

  Test the action of the enzyme in saliva on a 0.5% starch solution made up in a 0.25% sodium chloride solution. After mixing the starch with enzyme, check at regular intervals for any remaining starch by adding a few drops of Lugol's iodine. In the presence of starch, Lugol's iodine turns blue-black. Record the time and continue testing until no color change is evident. Use a computer program to prepare a graph that shows the rate of the reaction versus the concentration of the saliva.

- Rather than using the enzyme in liver or saliva, isolate a different enzyme from either an animal or a plant. Because isolating an enzyme can be difficult, you may want to work with extracts from a plant or an animal. For example, mix a small plant with some sand and water in a mortar. Grind it with a pestle until you form a paste. Filter the paste through cheesecloth to collect the liquid extract. If this extract shows enzymatic activity, experiment with various ways to influence its action.

- Some enzymes require other chemicals to function. These chemicals are called coenzymes. Some salts and vitamins have been shown to work as coenzymes. Plan a project to see whether your enzyme works better if another chemical is present. On the other hand, enzyme action can be inhibited by certain chemicals. For example, penicillin inhibits the action of a bacterial enzyme. Design an experiment to identify an inhibitor for your enzyme.

- If you tested the effects of temperature changes, you probably discovered an optimum range for enzyme action. However, not all enzymes function best in this range. For example, the characteristic color of a Siamese cat depends on enzymes that become active only at low temperatures. This enzyme controls the production of the dark pigment in the face, ears, and paws.

  Plan a project to see what other animals have enzymes that are affected by temperature changes. Work with a small animal normally found in either a

Two Siamese cats

very warm or very cold climate. Look for any changes in physical appearance as you alter the temperature. If any occur, prove that they are the result of enzyme action. By the way, if you plan to enter your project in a science fair, check on regulations regarding the use of animals. Many science fairs either prohibit experiments with vertebrates or have strict guidelines on their use.

• If working with small animals is a problem, you can conduct a number of projects with enzymes by using *microorganisms*. Lysozyme is an enzyme found in the tears, saliva, milk, and many other fluids of different animals. This enzyme breaks down the wall surrounding a bacterial cell. Try to detect lysozyme by adding small drops of various fluids to bacteria growing on agar cultures. If lysozyme is present, the bacteria will be destroyed and replaced by a clear area on the plate. You can extend this project by analyzing the various lysozymes to see what amino acids they have in common.

CHAPTER 3

CELL STRUCTURE AND FUNCTION

Scientists believe that Earth is about 4.6 billion years old. Early in our planet's history, the atmosphere and surface were very unstable. Violent thunderstorms occurred frequently, and strong winds swept across the land. Volcanoes erupted from the ocean floor, and cosmic radiation from the Sun scorched Earth's surface. Amid such turbulence, early life forms appeared.

Scientists disagree about how life came to exist on Earth. According to one theory, it all began when chemical compounds started to collect and mix in places where they were not smashed apart by the action of the oceans or destroyed by radiation from the Sun. Perhaps these chemicals accumulated in tiny pools of water.

Scientists believe that the chemicals involved in that first step included various gases released into the atmosphere by the volcanic eruptions. These gases are classified as *inorganic compounds*. With just a few exceptions, inorganic compounds are substances that do not contain the element carbon. Gradually these inorganic gases were assembled in the presence of water and energy to form larger, organic compounds. At first these organic compounds were simple. Amino acids, the building blocks of proteins, were probably among the first organic compounds on Earth.

The theory goes on to say that, over millions of years, more complex organic compounds formed, including proteins, carbohydrates, and lipids. Scientists have been able to make a number of these organic compounds in their labs, starting with just the inorganic materials thought to have been present on the primitive Earth.

Did some of the more complex organic compounds combine to create the first living cells? This is a question that scientists can't answer. No one has been able to accomplish this step in a laboratory setting. However, scientists have found ways to make proteins form organized structures called *microspheres*. Using various organic compounds, scientists have also been able to create tiny droplets known as *coacervates*.

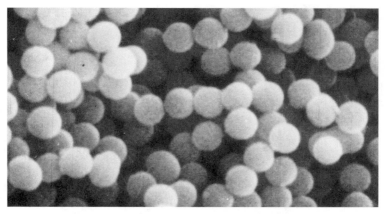

This photograph of microspheres was
taken through a microscope.

MICROSPHERES AND COACERVATES

Although microspheres and coacervates are not living organisms, they exhibit many of the characteristics of cells. For example, molecules at the edge of these structures form a protective coat much like a cell's membrane. The outer layer protects internal molecules from the surrounding environment. These structures may have been the precursors of the first living cells.

FORMING A COACERVATE

What You Need	
Test tube	Dropper
Graduated cylinder	Glass microscope slides
1% gelatin solution	Coverslips
1% gum arabic solution	Microscope
0.1 N HCl*	

In a test tube, mix 3 mL of the gelatin solution with 5 mL of the gum arabic solution. Gelatin is a protein, while gum arabic is a carbohydrate. Add the 0.1 N HCl drop by drop. *Caution: HCl is a dangerous acid. Work in a well-ventilated area and wear safety goggles, gloves, and an apron or a smock. You may want to work under the supervision of an adult. If so, be sure that the adult also*

---

* The N represents normality—a unit used to denote the concentration of a solution.

follows these safety precautions. Gently shake the solution after adding each drop. Continue adding the acid until the solution turns cloudy. Place one drop of the solution on a glass microscope slide. Why is it especially important not to trap any air bubbles when you place a coverslip on the slide? Examine the solution under the highest-power magnification of a microscope. Look for coacervates.

Doing More

- You can make protein microspheres by mixing powders of different amino acids. Start by mixing 1 g each of five different amino acids. Place the powdered mixture in an Erlenmeyer flask. Next, suspend the flask in a beaker of boiling water so that the amino acids are heated for at least 20 minutes.

   While the amino acids are being heated, add 10 mL of a 1% NaCl solution to a small Erlenmeyer flask and bring it to a boil. Using tongs, carefully pour the hot 1% NaCl solution into the hot amino acids while stirring. Boil the NaCl-amino acid solution for 30 seconds. Allow the solution to cool and examine a drop of the solution under a microscope.

   Experiment to see what kinds of microspheres you can assemble by varying the amino acids you use. What conditions are best suited for assembling these microspheres? Compare acidic versus basic conditions and salt solutions other than NaCl.

- Some scientists are working to develop microspheres that can be used to deliver certain drugs into the human body. The microspheres release prescribed quantities of drugs for specific amounts of time. Such microspheres avoid the need for repeated injections or multiple pills that must be taken every day.

These microspheres are most useful for drugs that patients need continuously or frequently. Examples include insulin, which is used to treat diabetes, and growth hormone, which is taken for dwarfism. Microspheres are also being developed to deliver multiple drugs taken in either tablet or capsule form. One day microspheres may even be used to deliver drugs that would boost the immune systems of people with HIV infection or AIDS.

Research the use of microspheres in drug delivery. Designing and completing a project that develops a new drug-delivering microsphere may have wide-reaching impact. You will need to consider the chemical interaction between the drug and microsphere, drug dosage, a mechanism of controlled release, and a site-specific delivery system. You may want to investigate the development of microspheres aimed at masking the unpleasant taste of certain drugs that are taken by mouth, including cold and cough medications.

THE EARLIEST CELLS

As time passed, microspheres and coacervates became more and more complex. Eventually, they developed the ability to produce offspring. The ability to reproduce is a requisite for something to be considered living. Over time, microspheres and coacervates could have evolved into cells—the basic unit of structure and function of all living things. In the following project, you can compare the structure of cells from all "walks of life."

COMPARING CELL STRUCTURES

Gently scrape the lining of your mouth with a flat edge of a toothpick to remove cheek cells. Wipe the flat edge back and forth across a microscope slide. Add a drop of

What You Need	
Toothpick	Potato
Glass microscope slides	Mushroom
Methylene blue stain	Pond water
Plastic cup of water	Dropper
Paper towels	Sterile petri dish with nutrient agar
Coverslips	
Microscope	Sterile cotton swab
Sharp knife or scalpel	Bleach

methylene blue stain. *Caution: Be careful when using methylene blue. It can irritate your eyes and stain your clothes and skin.* Allow the stain to remain on the slide for 2 minutes and then dip it into a plastic cup of water several times. Blot the slide with a paper towel, being careful not to rub the slide. Allow the slide to dry. Place a coverslip on the slide. Examine your cheek cells under a microscope. Cheek cells are typical of those found in animals. Compare your cheek cells to those shown in the photo on the next page. Note the similarities and differences.

Use a sharp knife or scalpel to cut a paper-thin section of a potato. Prepare a slide as described above, and observe it under a microscope. Potato cells are typical of those found in plants. Compare your potato cells to your cheek cells. How do animal and plant cells differ?

Use a sharp knife or scalpel to cut a paper-thin section of a mushroom. Prepare a slide as described above, and observe it under a microscope. Mushroom cells are typical of those found in fungi. Compare the mushroom

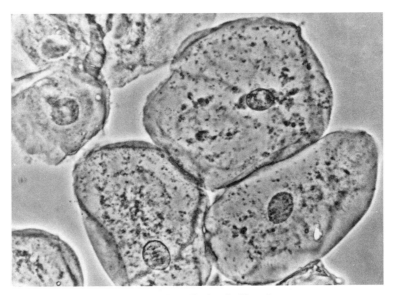

Do your cheek cells look like the ones
shown in this photograph?

cells to the cheek and potato cells. How do the fungi cells
differ from those of plants and animals?

Prepare a *wet mount* of a drop of pond water. Look for
unicellular, or one-celled, organisms. These one-celled
organisms belong to a group of living things called protists. How do their cells compare to those of fungi, plants,
and animals?

Remove the cover from a sterile petri dish containing
nutrient agar. Expose the agar to the air for 10 minutes.
Cover the dish and place it in a warm, dark area for several days. Look for any organisms that start to grow on the
agar. They will appear as circular regions called colonies.
Each colony represents millions of bacteria. These bacteria grew from bacteria that landed on that spot when the
agar was exposed to the air. *Caution: Do not touch the
colonies. Some of the bacteria might cause disease.*

Use a sterile swab to transfer a very small amount of the colony to a microscope slide. Spread the bacteria on the slide and allow it to dry. Stain the bacteria with methylene blue as described above, add a coverslip, and examine the sample under a microscope. Check with your science teacher to see whether an oil immersion lens is available.* Because of their extremely small size, bacterial cells are difficult to see. Take the time to note similarities and differences between these cells and the ones you looked at earlier.

When you are finished using the agar dish, cover the surface with liquid bleach, and soak it for 24 hours. Carefully rinse the agar dish with running water, and dispose of it properly.

Prepare a report summarizing all your observations. A computer drawing program could be used to create illustrations of the different cell types you have observed. Include a table that lists the similarities and differences between the cell types.

Doing More
- Compare unstained specimens of cells by using different types of microscopes. Use a phase-contrast, differential-interference, or dark-field microscope. These microscopes reveal features that are difficult to detect with an ordinary light microscope. If you are interested in photography, mount a camera to the body tube of the microscope and take pictures of your specimens. You can also attach a video camera to a microscope to tape the action of live cells. A careful analysis of the videotape might reveal some interesting aspect of a cell's structure.

---

* Combined with the use of a special oil, this lens provides a higher magnification, making it easier to see the bacteria.

- Microscopes that use electrons rather than light to form images reveal much more detail about the structure of cells. The transmission electron microscope (TEM) can magnify an image up to 200,000 times. The scanning tunneling microscope (STM) provides three-dimensional images of the structures that make up a cell.

  Both types of electron microscopes have provided a wealth of information about the internal structure of cells, but much remains to be learned. For example, scientists are probing the structure that helps a cell maintain its shape and size. Known as the cytoskeleton, this structure functions like the skeleton of your body.

  One of the most active areas of research on the cytoskeleton centers on its role in neurodegenerative diseases. These are diseases in which nerve cells break down and die, such as Alzheimer's disease and Parkinson's diseases. Search the Internet for information about these neurodegenerative diseases. You may come up with an idea for a project.

  For additional ideas, contact scientists at a local university or research laboratory that has an electron microscope. Volunteer to help with one of their projects. Once you understand the workings of the microscope, you might be able to design and carry out a project on your own.

- Obviously, all the cells you examined are microscopic. In fact, only a few types of cells, such as red blood cells, are visible to the unaided eye. You can conduct a project that examines what limits the size of cells.

  Use heavy, colored paper to prepare models of different-sized cells. All the cells should be cube-shaped, starting with one that measures 1 cm on each side.

Leave one side open so that you can fill the "cell" with sand. You must calculate the surface area/volume and surface area/weight ratios of each cell. The surface area represents how much *cell membrane* each "cell" has. The volume and weight represent how much "stuff" each "cell" contains.

What happens to the surface area/volume and surface area/weight ratios as the cell gets larger? How might this affect the functioning of a cell? Design and carry out an experiment to test your hypothesis, using either real cells or cell models.

THE CELL MEMBRANE

Were you surprised by the differences between the cells you observed in the previous project? Despite their differences, all cells share certain characteristics. For example, all cells are surrounded by a cell membrane. The cell membrane, also known as the plasma membrane, controls what enters and leaves the cell.

Because cell membranes allow only certain substances to pass through them, they are said to be semipermeable. You can study what controls the movement of materials across the cell membrane in the following project.

CONTROLLING WHAT ENTERS
AND LEAVES A CELL

Caution: Put on your protective eye goggles before beginning this procedure. In a beaker, dissolve some sugar, starch, salt, and gelatin (protein) in distilled water. Pour the solution into a piece of dialysis tubing, which will serve as a cell membrane. (Dialysis tubing contains pores that allow certain substances to pass in and out.) Insert a 10-mL pipette into one end of the tubing, and place it in a second beaker of distilled water, as shown in Figure 2. Record the height of the water in the pipette after placing the dialysis tubing in the water. After 30 minutes, again record the height of the water in the pipette. Explain any difference that you observe in the height of the water.

Test the contents of the beaker and dialysis tubing for sugar (with a test strip), starch (with Lugol's iodine), salt (with 5% silver nitrate), and protein (with Biuret reagent). *Caution: Be careful when using these chemicals; they may irritate your skin.*

If you need additional instructions, ask your science teacher for guidance. Based on your results, determine which substances crossed the membrane. Explain why only certain substances can diffuse through the membrane.

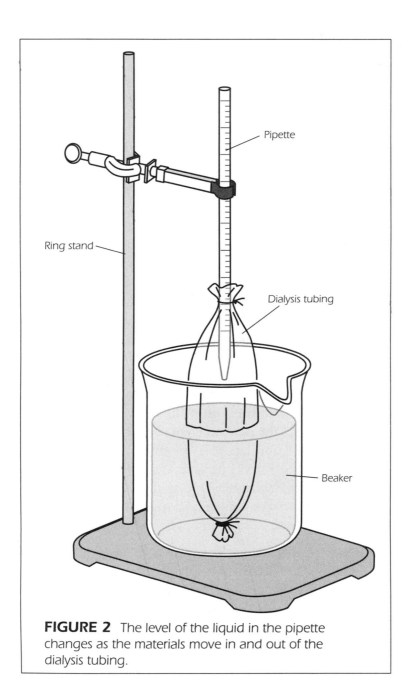

FIGURE 2 The level of the liquid in the pipette changes as the materials move in and out of the dialysis tubing.

Pipette

Ring stand

Dialysis tubing

Beaker

Doing More

- Experiment with other chemicals to test whether they can pass through the membrane. Explore ways of changing a substance that cannot diffuse so that it will pass through the membrane. Try heating or exposing the chemical to enzyme action. Test the effects of boiling water, exposure to mild acids or bases, and stretching to see whether you can alter the permeability of the dialysis tubing.

- Diffusion and osmosis across a cell membrane involve concentration gradients. Carry out a project that examines how different concentrations of a substance affect diffusion and osmosis. You can use different concentrations of the same solution, and pour equal volumes into a piece of dialysis tubing. For example, you can pour 20 mL each of 1.0 M, 0.8 M, 0.6 M, 0.4 M, and 0.2 M sucrose solutions into five separate dialysis bags. Determine the weight of each bag before and after immersing it in distilled water. Any weight change is due to the gain or loss of water.

  Calculate the percent change in the weight of each bag. Graph your data plotting molarity (the independent variable) versus percent change (the dependent variable). Use substances other than sucrose to determine whether the concentration gradients for all substances behave in the same way.

- Water moves through dialysis tubing as a result of osmosis. Any other substance that passes through the tubing does so as a result of diffusion. Osmosis and diffusion are not the only mechanisms by which substances pass through the cell membrane. Other processes include facilitated diffusion, active transport, endocytosis, and exocytosis.

Much remains to be learned about these processes. For example, diabetes is a disease that results from the failure of cells to take up sugars, mainly glucose, by the process of active transport. Insulin given by injection to those with diabetes stimulates body cells, especially muscles, to absorb glucose. To get an idea for a project involving the role of active transport in diabetes, contact the American Diabetes Association (*http://www.diabetes. org*). This home page has links to a number of sites, including one that provides the latest information on diabetes research.

- Plant cells, especially those in the roots, must use active transport to obtain the salts needed for growth. Active transport is a process in which substances are moved from an area of lower concentration to one of higher concentration. Unlike diffusion and osmosis, active transport requires energy to operate. You can use cells from an *Elodea* plant to study active transport. In light, cells on the undersurface of their leaves actively uptake calcium from the water. The cells on the upper surface secrete any excess back into the environment.

  Prepare a saturated solution of calcium carbonate by dissolving as much of the salt as possible in tap water that has been allowed to sit for a few days. Standing will allow any unwanted gases in the water to escape into the atmosphere. Add a small amount of phenolphthalein. If the solution is pink, blow into it through a straw until it becomes colorless. Blowing into the solution adds carbon dioxide, which causes the solution to become colorless. Submerge a plant in this solution. If calcium salts are actively secreted by the cells on the upper surface of the leaf, the solution surrounding this area will become alkaline and turn pink because of the phenolphthalein. Add different salts to study their effect on active transport. Vary the salt concentrations, including that of calcium carbonate, to determine the point at which inhibition of active transport occurs. Can you identify the salt that is the most effective inhibitor? Do different light intensities and wavelengths affect active transport in plants?

- Regardless of whether the cell membranes are found in animals, plants, fungi, protists, or bacteria, scientists do not know how they carry out active transport. Some researchers believe that special proteins called carriers may be involved. These carriers pick up a substance on one side of the membrane and dump it on the other. Exactly how they accomplish this task is not clear, although scientists know active transport requires large amounts of energy. According to some estimates, more than one-third of the ATP used by a resting animal is used for active transport. Perhaps you can spend some of the remaining energy on a project to identify a carrier protein.

CELL DIVISION

One of the most important functions of cells is dividing to produce new cells. There are two mechanisms by which cells divide. One mechanism is called *mitosis*. The other mechanism, *meiosis*, will be discussed in Chapter 6. During mitosis, one cell divides to produce two cells that have the identical genetic material as the original cell. In many organisms, the genetic material is located in the cell's *nucleus*. The nucleus acts as the control center of a cell, directing most of its activities. The following project looks at the various stages of mitosis.

OBSERVING MITOSIS

What You Need	
Onion or garlic	Matches
A container with water	Paper towels
Scalpel or sharp knife	Toluidine blue O or aceto-orcein stain
Glass microscope slides	
1 N HCl	Coverslips
Bunsen burner	Microscope

Place an onion or a garlic bulb in a container with water. After the roots sprout, select one that is at least 3 cm long. Using a scalpel, cut off a section 1 cm from the bottom of the root. Place the tip on a clean glass microscope slide, and cover it with a few drops of 1 N HCl.

Caution: HCl is a dangerous acid. Work in a well-ventilated area and wear safety goggles, gloves, and an apron or a smock. You may want to work under the supervision of an adult. If so, be sure the adult also follows these safety precautions.

Pass the slide over a low flame two or three times. Using paper towels, blot off any remaining acid. Cover the tip with a few drops of toluidine blue O or aceto-orcein stain. Again pass the slide through the flame and blot it dry. Add a drop of fresh stain, apply a coverslip, and place the slide between two paper towels. Press gently with your thumb using a steady, firm pressure to crush the onion root tip. Examine the slide with a microscope. You

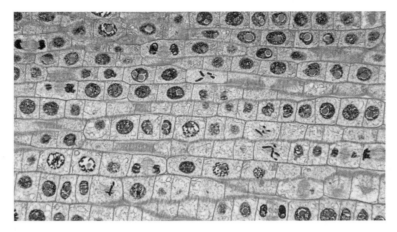

Many of the cells in this onion root show are dividing.
Can you see the chromosomes in some cells?

can also use a slide that has been prepared with a section of an onion root tip.

As you look at the onion root cells, notice the darkly stained structures near the center of the cells. These are the *chromosomes*. A chromosome is a rod-shaped structure that contains *deoxyribonucleic acid* (DNA). Individual chromosomes are not visible in most of the cells you will examine. These cells are in a stage that occurs between cell divisions. The cells that do contain visible chromosomes are undergoing mitosis.

Mitosis consists of four stages. During *prophase*, the chromosomes become visible. During *metaphase*, the chromosomes organize near the middle of the cell. During *anaphase*, the chromosomes move away from one another. During *telophase*, two distinct cells start to form. The stages of mitosis are shown in Figure 3.

Examine fifty cells that are undergoing mitosis. Identify the stage of mitosis for each cell. Keep a tally of your observations. In onion cells, mitosis takes about 80 min-

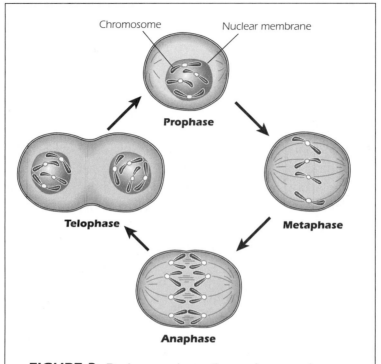

Chromosome   Nuclear membrane

Prophase

Telophase   **Metaphase**

Anaphase

FIGURE 3 During prophase, the nuclear membrane begins to break down and chromosome pairs are visible. During metaphase, the chromosome pairs line up along in the middle of the cell. During anaphase, the member of each chromosome pair move toward the opposite ends of the cell. During telophase, the cell begins to split into two new cells.

utes. You can calculate the length of a particular stage by multiplying the percentage of cells in that stage by 80. For example, if five of the fifty cells are in prophase, then the length of this stage would be calculated in the following manner:

$$5 \div 50 = 0.10$$
$$0.10 \times 80 = 8 \text{ minutes}$$

Doing More

- Prepare your slides at different times of the day to see whether there is a peak period for mitosis. Expose the onion or garlic to different light and temperature cycles. A project determining the optimum conditions for mitosis would have practical application for growing the plant.

- Experiment with ways of affecting cell division by adding various substances to the water used for rooting. Look for any obvious abnormalities: broken or damaged chromosomes, changes in their number, or irregular arrangements. Test the effects of such plant products as nicotine, caffeine, and quinine. Experiment with colchicine, a chemical that allows chromosomes to double but prevents the cell from dividing. As a consequence, the cell ends up with an extra set of chromosomes.

  Scientists have used colchicine to produce plants with larger flowers and fruits. Find out if any of these changes are reversible—can you restore the chromosomes to their original condition?

- In the early 1960s, scientists took small pieces of carrots and placed them in Erlenmeyer flasks containing a culture medium that included coconut milk. The flasks were sealed to prevent contamination and gently shaken. The carrot cells grew rapidly. Next, the scientists took individual carrot cells to grow in culture. The cells divided rapidly to form large fragments, which developed into small plants when transferred to agar containing coconut milk. These were the first cloning experiments, producing a complete organism from a single cell. A *clone* is an organism that is produced from a single cell and is genetically identical to its parent.

Carry out a project by cloning carrots, lettuce, or a fern plant. Begin by washing pieces cut from the plant in warm, soapy water. Rinse with sterile distilled water before placing the fragments in a 15% chlorine bleach solution. Shake the container for about 5 minutes. Rinse again with sterile distilled water. Place the plant section in a sterile petri dish containing nutrients and the plant hormone auxin. Expose the dishes to light 12 hours a day for 2 to 3 weeks. A solid mass of unspecialized cells called a *callus* will develop. Using sterilized forceps, remove a small piece of the callus. Place it in a test tube of gelatin containing nutrients and two plant hormones, auxin and cytokinin. This growth medium will cause the callus to grow into a fully developed plant.

Cloning experiments are often unsuccessful because of the constant need for sterile conditions and the difficulty of maintaining proper hormone combinations. You may find it worthwhile to begin a cloning project by using a kit purchased from a scientific supply company. Most of these companies do not sell directly to individuals, so you may have to ask your science teacher to order the kit for you. Once you have mastered the technique, try to develop ways to improve the method, or try it with other plants.

- Since the early 1960s, scientists have cloned a variety of organisms, but the technique is very controversial. In 1997, President Bill Clinton issued an order banning any federally funded project aimed at cloning humans. That same year, Italy, Denmark, and several other countries banned all cloning experiments.

Check the library and search the Internet for points of view on both sides of this issue. Cloning is just of one of several "bioethical" issues. For a project, you can prepare a position statement outlining your views on one of these issues. Be sure to support your position with facts and scientific knowledge. Your project can also take the form of a video documentary. Watching the movie *The Boys from Brazil* may give you ideas about how to proceed with the development of a story plot.

A LOOK
AT
MICROORGANISMS

Microorganisms are living things that are not visible to the unaided eye. They can be seen only with a microscope. All bacteria, most protists, and some fungi are microorganisms. Although invisible to the unaided eye, microorganisms thrive everywhere on Earth. In fact, bacteria are the most numerous organisms in the world. They can be found in the frozen Arctic, on the ocean bottom, and on everything you touch.

Most of what we know about microorganisms is the result of studying diseases. Bacteria cause such diseases as strep throat, tuberculosis, tooth decay, food poisoning, and tetanus. Protists can bring about malaria, severe diarrhea, sleeping sickness, skin sores, intestinal cramps, and severe heart damage. Fungi cause athlete's foot, vaginal infections, "jock itch," and ringworm.

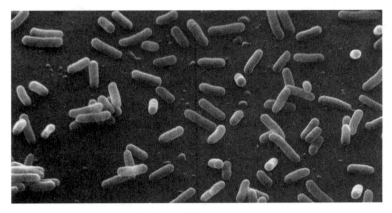

These *Salmonella* bacteria cause
some types of food poisoning.

But many microorganisms are beneficial to humans. Bacteria are used to treat raw sewage, make insecticides, and produce such foods as sour cream, yogurt, cottage cheese, sauerkraut, and pickles. The protists include algae, which are important food producers. Fungi, such as mushrooms, recycle materials by decomposing dead organisms. Fungi are also a source of drugs, including various antibiotics used to treat bacterial diseases.

BACTERIA: A CLOSER LOOK

Many scientists divide bacteria into two groups—archaebacteria and eubacteria. A growing number of researchers believe that archaebacteria were the first organisms to evolve on Earth. Rock deposits discovered in Australia appear to contain fossils of archaebacteria that existed on Earth almost 4 billion years ago. Today, archaebacteria are most common in extreme environments, such as the deep sea and hot springs. As a result, most of the bacteria you study will probably be eubacteria.

A bacterium is a unicellular organism. The cell is surrounded by a membrane. Unlike other creatures, a bacterium has no nucleus or other cellular structures. As a result, bacteria are called *prokaryotes*. Prokaryotes inhabited Earth for nearly 1 billion years before more complex cells, known as *eukaryotes*, evolved. The cells of a eukaryote contain a nucleus and other structures. During the nearly 4 billion years they have inhabited Earth, prokaryotes have successfully invaded a variety of environments. To find out more about the types of environments bacteria prefer, try the next project.

CULTURING BACTERIA

What You Need	
Piece of lean beef	Glass jars with narrow mouths
Beaker filled with water	
Bunsen burner or hot plate	Thermometer
	Cotton
Thermometer	Pressure cooker
Peptone	Refrigerator
Balance	Graduated cylinder or measuring cup
Distilled water	
	Stopwatch

To *culture*, or grow, the most bacteria in the shortest possible time, you should use special culture media. These media can include natural ingredients (blood, milk, eggs, animal tissues), synthetic combinations (including a variety of chemicals), and special preparations (materials processed from plants and animals). One of the most commonly used culture media is known as nutrient broth. Nutrient broth includes a chemical ingredient (peptone) and beef extract added to distilled water. You can purchase peptone or even the nutrient broth from a scientific supply company. Your science teacher can help you do this.

If you want to make your own nutrient broth, boil a piece of lean beef until it forms a thick paste. Nutrient broth is made by dissolving 5 g of peptone and 3 g of beef paste in 1 liter (L) of distilled water. Add these ingredients to a glass jar with a narrow mouth, and heat the mixture at 60°C until the ingredients dissolve.

To prevent unwanted growth of bacteria or other microorganisms in the broth, cover the glass jar with cotton and sterilize it for 25 minutes in a pressure cooker. Store the sterilized broth in a refrigerator until needed. Also sterilize all the glass containers you will use in the experiments described below.

Pour 100 mL of the nutrient broth into a sterile glass jar. Expose the broth to the air for 10 minutes, then stopper the opening with cotton. You can expose different 100 mL samples of your broth to the air in various locations to see which areas contain the most bacteria. Be sure that the location is the only independent variable. This includes making sure that the openings on all the jars are the same size. What additional variable would you be introducing if the openings were different sizes? What will be your control for this experiment?

After a few days, observe the broth and describe what you see in your notebook. Be careful not to spill or touch the broth because some of the bacteria growing in the flask may cause disease. When you are finished with the broths, sterilize them to kill the bacteria before pouring the solution down a drain.

- Observing protists under a microscope is not easy. Because they are so small and often move quickly, you must be patient and observe closely. Luckily, there are several ways to make your job easier.

    One way is to prepare a hanging-drop suspension. Place a drop of your sample on the center of a coverslip. Add a drop or two of water to the edge of the depression of a concave slide. Invert the coverslip and place it over the depression of the slide, as shown in Figure 4. The drops of water on the edge of the depression will help prevent the coverslip from sliding and also act like a seal so that the hanging drop will not evaporate. The protists will be easier to find in the small drop. Because the microorganisms will

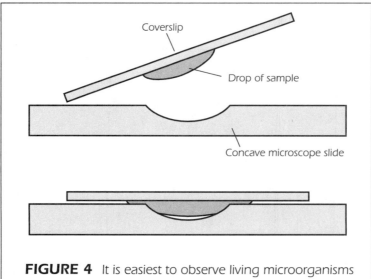

FIGURE 4 It is easiest to observe living microorganisms by preparing a hanging drop suspension using a concave microscope slide. Be sure to position the drop of sample so that it will fall into the depression on the slide when you gently lower the coverslip onto the slide.

not be squashed and killed by the coverslip, you can observe how they move.

Another way to make it easier to observe protists is with an oil immersion lens. Recall from Chapter 3 that this type of lens provides a higher magnification. If you use an oil immersion lens, be sure that the lens is in the oil and not touching the slide. Because the oil is quite thick, you will need to increase the amount of light striking the slide.

MICROFUNGI: A CLOSER LOOK

Although you may not realize it, you are familiar with many different kinds of fungi. This group includes the mold that grows on bread or oranges that have spoiled. The greenish fuzz that sometimes appears on the surface of spoiled foods is actually the fungus *Penicillium*. As the original source of the antibiotic penicillin, this fungus has been

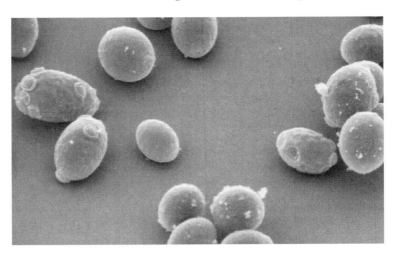

This photograph of yeast cells was taken through a microscope. The cells have been magnified about 6,000 times.

quite beneficial to humans. The greenish fuzz you see is the fungus's reproductive structures. The rest of the fungus consists of a tangled mass of cells inside the spoiled food.

Yeast is another fungus that is quite beneficial to humans. Yeast cells are added to some baked products, such as pizza and bread, to make the dough rise. Yeast contains enzymes that react with the carbohydrates in the dough. This chemical reaction produces carbon dioxide gas that causes the dough to rise.

USING YEAST TO OBSERVE A CHEMICAL REACTION

What You Need	
Glass jar	Measuring cup
Limewater or calcium oxide	Thermos bottle
	One-hole rubber stopper
Tablespoon	
Sugar	Glass tubing
Water	Baker's yeast

Fill the glass jar halfway with limewater.* Dissolve 4 tablespoons of sugar in 1 cup of water. Pour the sugar solution into the thermos bottle. Make sure the one-hole rubber stopper fits snugly into the mouth of the thermos, and

---

* You can prepare your own limewater by dissolving calcium oxide in water. Fill the jar halfway with water, and slowly add calcium oxide until no more dissolves.

insert the glass tubing through the hole in the stopper.* Be sure to position the tubing so that the end is not in contact with the sugar solution. Place the other end of the glass tubing in the jar containing limewater.

Remove the stopper and tubing. Add one-quarter of the package of baker's yeast to the sugar solution. Reinsert the stopper and glass tubing into the thermos. The other end of the glass tubing must be inserted below the level of the limewater in the jar. When yeast is added to the sugar solution, carbon dioxide will be produced. It will escape through the tubing and pass into the jar where it will react with the limewater. When the carbon dioxide reacts with the calcium oxide, a white solid called calcium carbonate is formed. Soon, the limewater will become cloudy. The more calcium carbonate produced, the cloudier the solution.

Experiment to see how varying the amount of sugar and baker's yeast affects the amount of carbon dioxide produced. As carbon dioxide forms, the temperature of the mixture in the thermos rises. Because the thermos insulates the reaction, the heat is retained. Modify your procedure to see how much carbon dioxide is produced if the reaction is not insulated. The rubber stopper prevents oxygen in the air from mixing with the sugar solution in the thermos. How much carbon dioxide is produced if the sugar solution and yeast react in the presence of oxygen?

Doing More
- Preservatives are added to foods to prevent their spoilage by fungi. One such preservative is propionic acid. Design and carry out an experiment that demon-

---

* The glass tubing will have to be bent twice to run between the thermos bottle and the jar of lime water. If you cannot find glass tubing that has already been bent, you will have to do it yourself. Your science teacher can show you how to accomplish this.

strates the effect of adding propionic acid to different foods. Can you identify another substance that is more effective than propionic acid in preventing food spoilage? Check chemistry references for the structure of propionic acid. You can test other chemical compounds that have similar structures. Remember that any substance you test must be safe to eat!

• Some fungi have an interesting living arrangement. They live together with a partner that carries out photosynthesis. The partner—usually a green alga (protist) or a special type of bacteria—provides the fungus with food. In return, the fungus provides its partner with moisture, shelter, and protection. One type of fungus-alga duo is called a lichen. Lichens slowly decompose the rocks they grow on and return some of the materials to the soil.

Lichens can be used to identify sources of pollution. They were first recognized as potential indicators

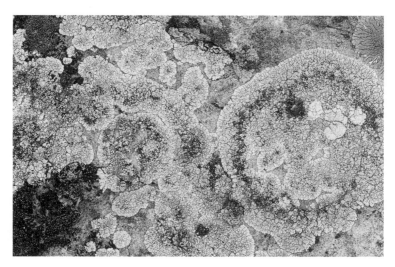

This lichen is growing on a rock
in a national park in Colorado.

of air pollution as early as the 1860s. Today, Finland leads the world in the use of lichens as pollution detectors. By studying the changes in lichens, scientists are able to identify the source of pollution hundreds of kilometers away. Such changes include the breakdown of chlorophyll; leakage of materials through the cell membranes; reduced photosynthetic, respiratory, and reproductive activity; and accumulation of toxic elements. Check the Internet for information on how lichens are used for such a purpose. Many of the lichens known to be sensitive to pollutants are the fruticose (hairlike) and foliose (leafy) lichens. Design and carry out an experiment that uses one of these lichens to identify a pollution source in your area.

- Without fungi, Earth would be vastly different. Only a few plants would be able to survive. More than 90 percent of all plants rely on a kind of fungi known as *mycorrhizae* to help them absorb materials through their roots.

  Mycorrhizae form a close association with the roots of plants. They absorb nutrients, especially phosphorus, and then transfer them to the host plant. A plant with mycorrhizae can absorb ten times more nutrients than a plant that lacks these fungi. Some plants, such as tomatoes, squash, asparagus, melons, grapes, and citrus trees, have thick, fleshy roots. Without mycorrhizae, the roots of these plants might not be able to absorb enough nutrients to live. Select one example of such a relationship between a mycorrhiza and a plant and investigate how the two interact. Determine exactly how materials are exchanged between the fungus and the plant.

CHAPTER 5

BODY SYSTEMS

One of the projects described in Chapter 2 suggests looking at why most cells are not very large. If you performed that project, you discovered that if a cell is too large, it cannot function because it does not have enough surface area (cell membrane) with respect to its volume (cell interior). The cell cannot function because it would take too long for some materials to diffuse deep into the cell's interior. Similarly, waste materials would have difficulty getting out of the cell. In both situations, the time needed would likely be so long that the cell would die.

That is why cells divide when they reach a certain size. In this way, they retain a surface area-to-volume ratio that permits diffusion of all materials within a reasonable amount of time. This explains why unicellular organisms are, for the most part, microscopic. All large organisms are multicellular. The average human body may consist of as many as 100 trillion cells.

Organisms with a large number of cells can divide the different tasks required to stay alive among their various cells. For example, certain cells may be specialized for digestion, others for respiration, and still others for circulation. In contrast, a unicellular organism must perform all its life functions within the contents of its single, non-specialized cell.

Cells that are organized to share a particular function are called a *tissue*. In turn, different tissues are assembled to form an *organ*. Various organs work together to make up a *system*. A multicellular organism is a medley of biological systems working together to carry out all its life functions. This chapter contains projects that deal with the systems that make up many organisms, including humans.

THE DIGESTIVE SYSTEM

In multicellular organisms, the digestive system breaks down food materials into smaller pieces so that they can be absorbed and used by individual cells. In many organisms, the digestive process involves two stages. First, food materials are broken down while they are still outside the organism's cells. Then the smaller particles are absorbed by each cell where they are broken down even further. The former process is called *extracellular digestion*, while the latter is known as *intracellular digestion*. In humans, extracellular digestion takes place in the mouth and stomach. To find out more about both digestive processes, try the next project.

FEEDING AN ANIMAL

Hydra are closely related to sea jellies. They are freshwater animals that live in still waters, such as ponds and lakes. They attach themselves to rocks or aquatic plants by secreting a sticky substance at the base. *Hydra* use their long tentacles to capture prey.

Place several *Hydra* in a watch glass filled approximately halfway with pond water. Tap water that has been allowed to stand is also suitable. Observe the *Hydra* with a stereomicroscope.

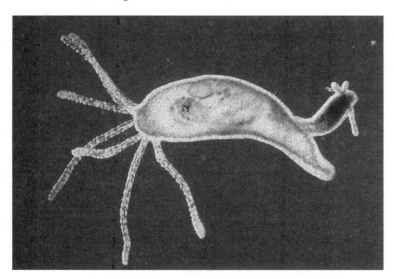

A *Hydra* catches prey with the tentacles located at one end of its body.

Hydra devour small organisms, such as *Daphnia*, which are relatives of crabs and crayfish. Once a *Hydra*'s tentacles are fully extended, place several drops of the liquid containing *Daphnia* near the tentacles. Observe what happens. Make sketches as the *Hydra* uses its tentacles to capture a *Daphnia*. The *Hydra* will use its tentacles to paralyze the *Daphnia* and then move the prey into its digestive cavity. As the *Hydra* does this, the digestive cavity will swell. Within its cavity, the *Hydra* will carry out extracellular digestion.

Once the *Daphnia* has been digested into small enough pieces, the *Hydra* will begin absorbing them into its cells. Once inside the cells, intracellular digestion will begin. This process is similar in *Hydra* and humans.

To expand upon this project, design an experiment to determine how *Hydra* detected *Daphnia:* Do *Hydra* use a visual, tactile, or chemical mechanism? If visual, the *Hydra* must somehow "see" its prey. If tactile, the *Hydra* must make physical contact with it. If chemical, the *Hydra*

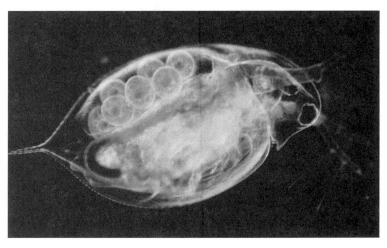

A *Daphnia* is transparent, so we can see the organs inside its body.

will respond to *Daphnia* that has been crushed into very small pieces.

Also try to observe the fine threads that *Hydra* shoot out from some of their cells to paralyze their prey. These threads can be seen in nematocysts that have discharged. If possible, use a phase-contrast microscope to observe discharged nematocysts. This type of microscope affects the light that strikes the specimen so that the contrast is increased, making it easier to see small structures.

If you add dilute acetic acid (vinegar) to the *Hydra* sample, their nematocysts will discharge. Determine where the nematocysts are concentrated on the *Hydra*. Investigate other ways of activating the nematocysts. For example, add various salts to the water, alter the light intensity, change the temperature, or test the effects of different chemicals found in your home, such as aspirin, bleach, and baking soda. Determine whether *Hydra* discharge additional nematocysts while they are in the process of eating.

Experiment with ways of preventing the discharge of nematocysts, even when food is present. Use a sharp scalpel to remove some of the tentacles. Add poisons, metals, alcohol, or aspirin to the water. Find out what other kinds of organisms *Hydra* will eat. Do plants or microorganisms, such as yeast, produce a feeding response? Prepare a report summarizing your findings about digestion in *Hydra*.

Doing More

- You can also study extracellular digestion in *Planaria*, sea urchins, snails, earthworms, crayfish, fiddler crabs, and barnacles. Compare the various methods of extracellular digestion used by these organisms. Include a study of food preferences. Present each organism with a variety of foods. Be sure to test each food sample with a sufficient number of organisms. Do these animals respond differently to living and dead food samples? Test the effect of freezing on the attractiveness of food. Experiment with food materials that have strong odors or vibrant colors.

- You may be surprised to learn that some plants, including the Venus flytrap, sundew, and pitcher plant, carry out extracellular digestion. Known as carnivorous plants, they secrete enzymes that digest insects, worms, and even larger animals, including birds and frogs. These plants are usually found in acidic soils where nitrogen is in low supply. Scientists

The leaves of a Venus flytrap can close quickly to trap insects. Then this amazing plant slowly digests its prey.

believe these plants compensate for the lack of nitrogen in the soil by obtaining it from their prey. Tiny electrodes placed in the tentacles extending from sundew leaves have detected electrical activity when the plant comes in contact with an insect. Scientists believe that electrical impulses, much like those sent through the nerves of animals, close the leaves and trap the insect. Carnivorous plants may use electrical signals to coordinate other body processes. Design a project to explore the mechanisms other carnivorous plants use to trap their prey. Investigate whether such mechanisms are used for other plant activities.

- Digestion in humans is a complex process. Three major classes of organic compounds are digested—proteins, lipids, and carbohydrates. Several organs are involved, either directly or indirectly. For example, the stomach begins the digestion of proteins, and the liver contributes to the digestion of lipids by producing bile. One possibility for a project is the development of a computer program that models the human digestive system. Such a program could be used to teach others how the digestive system operates.

    Once you understand how the human digestive system functions, you can begin designing your program. The program might follow the steps by which the three types of organic compounds are broken down and absorbed by the cells of the small intestine. For example, starting with carbohydrates, you could show how extracellular digestion begins in the mouth and is completed in the small intestine to produce glucose. Structures and organs involved would include the teeth, tongue, salivary glands, small intestine, and pancreas. Next, you could show what happens to the glucose after it is absorbed by the small intestine.

respiratory system, such as the nose and lungs, are responsible for obtaining oxygen from the environment. Like nutrients, oxygen is delivered to each cell by the circulatory system. In addition, the circulatory system delivers carbon dioxide to the respiratory system so that it can be eliminated from the body.

In the following project, you will be able to observe the process of respiration in either a hamster or a mouse. If you are looking for a science fair project, get a copy of the rules and guidelines before beginning this project. Many science fairs do not allow projects that involve mammals.

MEASURING OXYGEN UPTAKE

What You Need	
Mouse or hamster	Glass and rubber tubing
Large glass jar	Syringe
Tape	Food coloring
Thermometer	Soda lime
Piece of wire screen	Metric ruler

A respirometer measures the amount of oxygen an animal uses for respiration. You can construct a respirometer using the equipment listed above. Use Figure 6 as a guide. As the animal uses oxygen, the air pressure in the jar of the respirometer will fall. The higher pressure outside the jar will force the food coloring in the tube toward the container. By measuring the distance traveled by the liquid in a given time, you can determine the animal's rate of oxygen uptake.

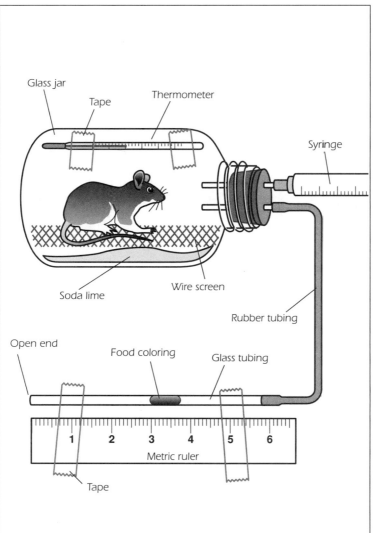

Glass jar

Tape

Thermometer

Syringe

Soda lime

Wire screen

Rubber tubing

Open end

Food coloring

Glass tubing

1 2 3 4 5 6

Metric ruler

Tape

FIGURE 6 You can use a respirometer to measure the amount of oxygen an animal uses under various conditions. The soda lime absorbs the carbon dioxide given off by the animal. Add the food coloring to the open end of the glass tubing.

Examine how exercise affects the amount of oxygen the animal uses. First determine how much oxygen the animal normally uses by placing it in the respirometer. Repeat this process several times to obtain as accurate a measurement as possible. *Caution: Be sure to release the animal from the respirometer if it shows any signs of distress. It may not be getting enough oxygen.*

Next, determine how much oxygen the animal uses after having exercised. After the animal performs some sort of sustained activity, such as running on a wheel, place it in the respirometer. Determine whether the exercise affected the amount of oxygen used.

Can you identify other factors that affect respiration? Try manipulating the animal's diet. You can vary the amount of food you provide and the times of day you feed your animal. Check with someone at a pet store to see what different kinds of food can be given to your animal. Using the respirometer, find out whether altering the animal's diet affects the amount of oxygen it uses.

If possible, test more than one type of animal. For example, compare the oxygen used by mice and hamsters under the same exercise conditions. You may even want to design and construct a computer peripheral device that automatically displays and records the quantity of oxygen used.

Doing More
- Respiration can also be measured by monitoring carbon dioxide production. To do this, pour 100 mL of tap water into a clean flask. Breathe into the water through a straw for 1 minute. Add 5 drops of phenolphthalein. Record how much 0.4% sodium hydroxide solution you must add to turn this solution a light pink color. After subtracting the amount needed to turn tap water pink, multiply the milliliters of sodium

hydroxide added to your test solution by 10. This is the amount of carbon dioxide produced. Your answer will be expressed in a unit called micromoles.

Record the amount of carbon dioxide you produce after performing several different activities. Possibilities include sleeping, sitting, mild and vigorous exercise, or taking a test. Sample several classmates to see how much variation exists between people. Compare athletes with the rest of the class. Compare your results from different weight groups and ages. On average, does one gender produce more carbon dioxide?

- Most students mistakenly believe that the oxygen they breathe in turns into the carbon dioxide they breathe out. In fact, the oxygen used in respiration becomes part of the body's water.

  Scientists have not worked out all the details of the process by which oxygen is converted to water during respiration. Many of the unknown details involve the electron transport system, where most ATP is synthesized. One such detail involves something called a proton pump. Search the Internet for information on proton pumps. You might want to build a model or develop a computer simulation that demonstrates how proton pumps operate in the electron transport system.

- You may be surprised to learn that oxygen can be harmful, or even lethal, to some organisms. For example, certain bacteria are killed by the presence of oxygen. Even organisms that need oxygen to live often suffer harmful effects if oxygen pressure is too high. These effects include abnormal growth patterns, paralysis, and even death. Undertake a project to study the effects of increased oxygen pressure on organisms. Insects are suitable for this study.

You will need a sealed chamber capable of maintaining both an increased gas pressure and a temperature range between 25°C and 30°C. Ask your science teacher to help you find the proper equipment. Connect tanks of compressed oxygen, nitrogen, and air with pressure gauges to the chamber. ***Caution: Be sure to work under proper supervision because care should be taken when using gases under pressure.*** Your study may have some useful application for deep-sea divers and pilots who are exposed to varying oxygen pressures.

THE EXCRETORY SYSTEM

As a cell carries out its normal biological processes, it generates waste products. These products are often toxic. Thus, they must be either rendered harmless or eliminated as quickly as possible. The task of eliminating waste products falls to the excretory system. A multicellular organism excretes a number of waste products, including carbon dioxide, water, and nitrogen-containing substances. Because this last waste product is extremely poisonous, as much as possible must be eliminated. Aquatic organisms secrete nitrogen-containing wastes in the form of ammonia, which can be quickly washed away by the surrounding water. All birds and insects excrete nitrogen-containing wastes as uric acid, a concentrated substance that contains little water. Most mammals eliminate nitrogen waste products as urea, the main component of urine.

In mammals, the most important excretory organ is the kidney. The kidney operates according to the principle of *negative feedback*. According to this principle, if the concentration of a certain substance gets too high, the excess is eliminated in the urine. On the other hand, if the concentration of a certain substance falls too low, the kidney switches gears to conserve as much as possible until the level is brought back within the normal range.

Perhaps you have had your urine tested during a routine physical examination. A urinalysis provides information about how the organs of the body, especially the kidneys, are working. The cells of a kidney allow certain substances, but not others, to pass out of the body in the urine. In the case of a disease or an injury, however, certain substances that are not usually present may appear in the urine. The following project will allow you to conduct a simulated urinalysis.

ELIMINATING WASTES

What You Need	
Protective eye goggles	String
Glucose	Large glass jar
Albumin	Graduated cylinder
Balance	Sugar test strips
Large beaker	Protein test strip (or Biuret reagent)
Distilled water	
Yellow food coloring	Pin
Dialysis tubing	

Caution: Be sure to wear protective eye goggles while performing this procedure. Dissolve 5 g of glucose and 3 g of albumin in a beaker containing 100 mL of distilled water. Add several drops of the food coloring so that the solution has a distinct yellow color. Pour some of this solution into a 10-cm length of dialysis tubing that has been tied at one end with string. Tie off the open end and place the dialysis bag in a glass jar. Cover the dialysis bag with distilled water. The dialysis tubing represents the cell membranes of the cells that make up a kidney.

Allow the bag to remain submerged in the water for 24 hours. The next day, test the water in the beaker and the contents of the dialysis bag for sugar and albumin. If you use test strips, be sure not touch the strips with your fingers. Instead, place several drops of the sample directly on the test strip. Based on your results, explain your observations.

Sugar that appears in the urine is an indication that a person may be diabetic. Proteins are normally too large to diffuse across the cell membrane, so the presence of albumin indicates that the kidney may have been physically damaged. Repeat the procedure described above using a pin to punch a small hole in the dialysis bag before submerging it in the distilled water. How do the results differ from those you got originally?

Check with a local hospital or medical laboratory to find out what doctors can learn from an actual urinalysis. Extend your project to simulate as many of these conditions as possible. You can also set up artificial urine samples for others to analyze. Provide them with instructions for testing each sample and a table listing the various conditions that are possible if a test result is positive.

Doing More
- Because the kidneys play such an important role in eliminating toxic wastes, kidney failure can be life threatening. When a person's kidneys are not functioning properly, he or she may have to be placed on a dialysis machine. More than 100,000 people in the

United States suffer from kidney disease; most of them require periodic dialysis.

Check the library and search the Internet for information on kidney disease and dialysis. Two dialysis procedures are used—hemodialysis and peritoneal dialysis. In hemodialysis, a machine is used to filter the blood. In peritoneal dialysis, the body itself filters the blood. As part of your project, build working models or a computer simulation that shows how these two procedures are done.

- Excretion can also be studied with the help of earthworms. Inject an earthworm with a stain such as methylene blue. Then use a small amount of ether to anesthetize it. Search the library or the Internet for information on how to dissect an earthworm. When you cut open the earthworm, you will see that its excretory system consists of tubules called nephridia. The stain should help you locate the nephridia. Remove a few nephridia and observe them under a dissecting microscope. Look for cilia, hairlike projections that move waste products to the outside of the body. Are any of them still moving? Design a project to explore excretion in the earthworm. Use the movement of the cilia as an indication of excretory action.

THE CONTROL SYSTEMS

The systems that make up an organism cannot operate in a haphazard fashion. They must work as a unit for an organism to function efficiently. For example, cells should not absorb glucose for respiration unless they need the sugar. Similarly, cells should not produce enzymes for digestion unless food is present. The task of coordinating the various systems falls to the nervous system and the endocrine system.

Among its other responsibilities, the nervous system must detect and respond to stimuli, including light, odors, sounds, and touch. You may want to carry out a project to determine to what extent various organisms respond to these stimuli. For example, you could check whether a *Planaria*, a freshwater flatworm, prefers the light or dark, avoids chemicals that emit odors, curls up when touched, or reacts to vibrations. Vary the intensity of the different stimuli to see if the *Planaria* can detect changes to its environment. Repeat this procedure with a few different organisms. Compile a list of the organisms you tested, the stimuli you used, and the responses you detected. Can you make any conclusion that applies to all organisms tested? Pay particular attention to any unusual responses.

The endocrine system consists of glands located throughout the body. These glands secrete chemical substances called hormones. Hormones are chemicals that control the action of various organs or regulate biological processes. For example, one hormone can speed up the heart rate. Several other hormones control the level of sugar that circulates in the blood.

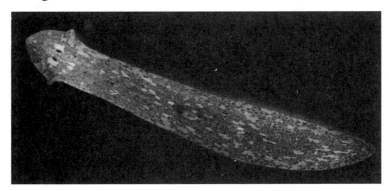

A *Planaria* is a type of flatworm.

You can carry out a project that investigates the effect of a hormone on some biological process, such as growth. For example, observe how tadpoles grow in the presence of varying concentrations of the hormone thyroxine, starting with a 0.01% thyroxine solution. Measure total length, body length, and tail length in tadpoles over a period of 3 to 4 weeks. Be sure to include the proper control and a controlled food source, such as boiled or strained spinach, for the growing tadpoles. Summarize your data by graphing your results.

GROWTH
AND
DEVELOPMENT

All multicellular organisms start out as a single cell. In animals, this single cell is known as a *zygote*. A zygote consists of a female's egg cell that has been fertilized by a sperm cell from a male. After the two cells have joined to produce a zygote, the single cell begins a series of mitotic divisions that eventually lead to the many cells that make up an organism. As you read earlier, on average, a human adult has some 100 trillion cells. How does a zygote—a simple, single cell—develop into a complex adult organism?

Although scientists have investigated this question for hundreds of years, they still do not have all the answers. But they do have some understanding of how development works. The cells that make up every organism have a set number of chromosomes. This number remains constant from one generation to the next. Recall from Chapter 3 that a chromosome is the structure within the

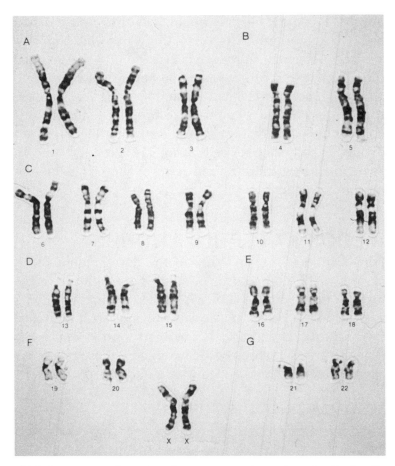

This karyotype is a visual representation of an individual's chromosomes arranged in a specific order.

nucleus of a cell that contains DNA, the hereditary information. With few exceptions, your cells contain forty-six chromosomes. The most notable exceptions to this rule are the egg cells in females and the sperm cells in males. If each of these cells had forty-six chromosomes, then a zygote would end up with ninety-two after fertilization. And this number would double every generation. In a relatively short time, humans would be nothing more than a bag of chromosomes. Obviously, this is not what happens.

Early scientists predicted that some process must occur to cut the chromosome number in half every time an egg or sperm is formed. Then, following fertilization, the original number would be restored. Eventually, scientists discovered that the chromosome number is indeed divided in half when sex cells form. This process is known as meiosis. Fertilization then restores the original chromosome number.

A LOOK AT FERTILIZATION

Fertilization is the first step in the development of an organism. This process can be studied in a variety of creatures. A most suitable choice is the sea urchin because its sperm and egg cells can be easily obtained without injury to the animal. In addition, because fertilization and development in sea urchins occur externally, these processes can be observed and studied with a microscope.

FERTILIZATION IN SEA URCHINS

What You Need	
Two pairs of protective eye goggles	Syringe with small needle
Sea urchins	Microscope
Seawater	Glass microscope slides
Small beaker or glass jar	Coverslips
0.5 M potassium chloride	Thermometer

Caution: Be sure to carry out this procedure under the supervision of an adult. Be sure that both of you wear protective eye goggles. Place a sea urchin, mouth side up, over a small beaker or glass jar filled with seawater. Inject 1 mL of 0.5 M potassium chloride solution into the soft tissues surrounding the mouthparts, as shown in Figure 7. After a few minutes, the sea urchin will release sex cells through small pores on the bottom of the animal. The eggs will be yellowish or clear, and the sperm will be white. Because you cannot determine the gender of a sea urchin by its external appearance, you may have to inject several of them before you find both a male and a female.

Observe egg and sperm cells separately under a microscope. Then prepare a slide containing both types of cells, and observe it under the microscope. Look for

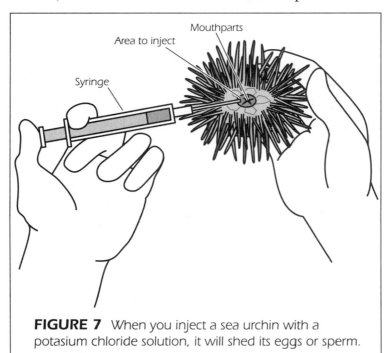

FIGURE 7 When you inject a sea urchin with a potasium chloride solution, it will shed its eggs or sperm.

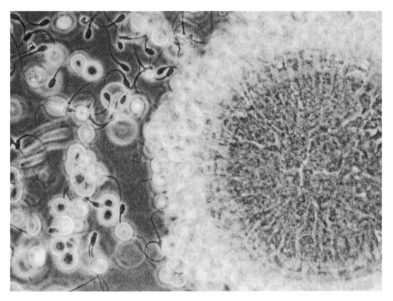

This photograph shows sperm cells swimming
around the edge of an egg cell.

sperm swimming against the egg in an attempt to fertilize it. If fertilization occurs, an impenetrable membrane will appear around the egg. This membrane will prevent other sperm from entering the egg. The zygote will begin its development into an adult sea urchin in about 1 hour. At this time, the zygote will divide by mitosis to form two cells.

Extend your project to observe the different stages of sea urchin development. Mix sperm and egg cells in a beaker of seawater. Try to maintain the seawater at as constant a temperature as possible—keep the beaker in a dark cabinet rather than near a window. Remove samples at periodic intervals for microscopic observation. Be sure to replace the seawater in the beaker with fresh seawater every other day. This will prevent the growth of other organisms, such as bacteria, that can kill the developing sea urchins.

Doing More

- Investigate the effects of temperature changes on fertilization and development. What happens when you vary the concentrations of sperm and egg cells? Expose the zygotes to radiation, ultraviolet light, or an electromagnetic field. Freeze the egg and sperm cells. Do these conditions effect their ability to undergo fertilization? What happens when you add various salt concentrations to the sex cells before freezing them?

- After sea urchin zygotes have divided into two cells, place them in a small vial filled with seawater. Shake the *embryos* gently to separate the two cells. Watch each cell as it develops into a normal, adult organism.

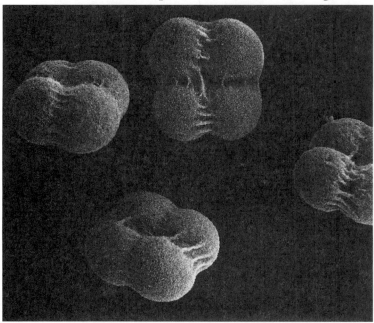

This photograph of four-celled sea urchin embryos was taken through a microscope. The cells have been magnified about 125 times.

Repeat the same process after the embryos have divided into four cells. Separate the cells of some embryos along the horizontal plane and others along the vertical plane. Do the sea urchins develop differently depending on how the eggs are separated? You can also separate the cells at different stages of development. Note how each organism develops.

• Sea urchins are sometimes difficult to obtain, especially if you do not live near the ocean or if you decide to begin your project in the middle of winter. In that case, you can study the development of frogs. Frogs are easier to obtain, even in winter. From October until April, each female frog contains about 2,000 eggs. In the spring, environmental conditions are just right to trigger the release of the eggs.

Scientists do not fully understand how changes in the environment cause a female frog to shed her eggs. Both the water temperature and the amount of sunlight are known to be important. Scientists know that the pineal gland, a small lobe of the brain, is responsible for detecting the amount of light present. In effect, the pineal gland acts as a biological timekeeper, not only in frogs but also in many other animals, possibly even in humans. Design a project to find out more about the role of the pineal gland in animal development.

If you are planning a project to study frog development, do not try to find a frog carrying mature eggs every time you need one. Instead, you can inject a pituitary preparation into a female's abdomen. Within 48 hours, you can check for eggs by grasping the female and gently squeezing her abdomen. The eggs will pour out when they are ready, as you can see in Figure 8.

Removing the pituitary glands to prepare the hormone injection is quite difficult, so you may want to order a frog ovulation kit—complete with pituitary extract, syringe, frogs, and instructions—from a science supply company. Your science teacher can help you do this. Directions for obtaining the sperm and fertilizing the eggs are included. When you have completed your project, be sure to release any tadpoles that develop into a pond or stream.

- The chicken egg has been used to study development for more than 300 years. It's a popular choice because it's large and readily available. Like all eggs, a chicken egg is a single cell. Its large size is the result of all the

FIGURE 8 When you gently squeeze the female frog's abdomen, her eggs will be forced out of her body.

yolk stored to feed the developing chick. Before doing the following project, make sure that you or someone you know will be able to feed and raise the chicks after they hatch.

Begin by getting an incubator and some fertilized eggs from a local farmer.* If there are no chicken farms nearby, ask your science teacher to help you order materials from a science supply company. The incubator will allow you to carefully monitor the temperature and humidity as the eggs develop.

To observe a chick as it develops, you will need to open a "window" in the egg. To do this, place the egg on a nest of paper towels that have been laid in a glass petri dish. If the egg is left undisturbed, the embryo will float to the top.

Use a sewing needle to scratch a rectangular area smaller than a glass coverslip on the egg's surface. Using forceps, break away small pieces of the shell until the embryo is exposed. See Figure 9.

To get a better look at the inside of the egg, use a hand lens or a stereomicroscope. After making a window in an egg, you can seal it by placing a coverslip over the opening and then sealing any openings with wax. *Caution: Be careful. Any hot wax dripped into the egg will kill the embryo.* You can observe the chick as it develops through this coverslip window.

One day after fertilization, the embryo will be a tiny white spot. In 14 days, feathers on the wings and legs will be visible. Note when other structures begin to appear. The chick will hatch in 21 days. Look for the development of four extraembryonic membranes

---

* The eggs sold in supermarkets are not fertilized because roosters are not allowed in the hen house!

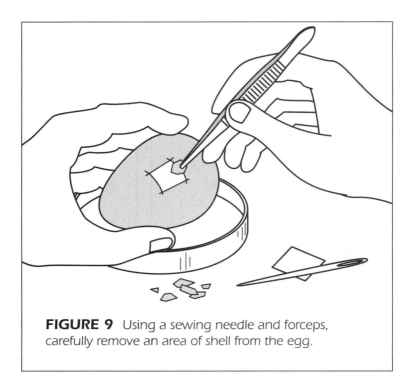

FIGURE 9 *Using a sewing needle and forceps, carefully remove an area of shell from the egg.*

not present in sea urchins or frogs. Compare chick development with that of other birds whose eggs are available. Make a table of your observations, recording both similarities and differences.

GROWTH

Although growth is part of the development process, it does not begin immediately following fertilization. First, a fertilized egg cell undergoes mitosis to produce two cells, both of which are the same size as the zygote. These two cells then divide, producing four cells. Each one is the same size as the original two cells. This process of cell division without growth occurs throughout the early stages of development. The cells of the developing organism start to grow later.

The process of growth can be easily observed in plants. The growth of a flowering plant begins with a seed. The seed consists of a tiny embryo, a supply of stored food, and a seed coat that protects the developing embryo. The stored food nourishes the embryo until the plant can begin making its own nutrients through photosynthesis. The following project investigates germination.

OBSERVING GERMINATION

Soak a bean seed and a corn kernel in water overnight. The next day, cut each one in half and observe them under a stereomicroscope. Compare the two seeds for similarities and differences. Identify the various parts of each seed by referring to a book on plants. Determine if starch is present by covering the cut seeds with Lugol's iodine.

Next, place six corn kernels along one end of a folded paper towel. Roll up the paper towel and secure it with a rubber band or string. Stand the towel in a beaker or a glass jar with some water in the bottom. Be sure that the end of the towel with the kernels is at the top, as shown in Figure 10 on page 106. The paper towel will soak up the water and keep the kernels moist. Keep the kernels moist for 3 days. Replace any water that evaporates from the glass jar. Repeat this procedure with six bean seeds.

After 3 days, remove the corn and bean seeds from the paper towels. Observe the roots and shoots that have started to grow. Starting at the seed, use a permanent marker and ruler to make a small dot every 0.5 cm along the shoot and

What You Need	
Bean seeds and corn kernels	Book on plants that includes a diagram of a seed
Small beakers or glass jars	Paper towels
Water	Rubber bands or string
Razor blade or sharp knife	Glass microscope slides
Stereomicroscope	Permanent marker
Lugol's iodine	Metric ruler

root. Rewrap the seeds in fresh paper towels, secure them with a rubber band, and place them in water.

After 3 more days have passed, remove the seeds from the paper towels. The first leaves that appear on a growing plant are called *cotyledons*. The cotyledons store food for the growing embryo. Measure the distance between the marks you made on the shoots and roots. In what region does growth occur in the shoot and in the root? Extend your project by examining the growth of other types of seeds. Note any similarities and differences you observe.

You can also investigate factors that can affect germination. Prepare a solution for soaking the paper towels that will double the rate of germination. You may also want to experiment with factors that will postpone germination. The seeds of most plants require a period of

library and search the Internet for information about that hormone. Design a project that involves a new application of the hormone.

REGENERATION

Many animals may develop normally, only to lose a body part in an accident or to a hungry predator. Some animals are able to replace or regenerate lost body parts. For years, people who liked to catch shellfish in coastal waters cut up sea stars and tossed them back into the ocean, thinking they would no longer have to compete with these creatures for clams and oysters. These people did not know that sea stars can regenerate lost body parts. By cutting up the sea stars, they were actually creating even more competition.

This sea star is regenerating one of its arms.

The sea star's ability to regenerate may be frustrating to shellfish lovers, but it is fascinating to many scientists. They know that if they can understand the mechanisms that allow sea stars to regenerate body parts, they may be able to find ways to regrow human body parts. Only a few structures in humans can regenerate. These include the skin and the liver. New skin is constantly regenerated to replace any that is lost in an injury. If a small portion of the liver is surgically removed to get rid of diseased tissue, the body can regenerate it. The following project will show you a *Planaria's* fantastic regenerative ability.

CUTTING UP A FLATWORM

What You Need	
Planaria	Stereomicroscope
Pond or tap water	Glass microscope slides
Razor blade or scalpel	Permanent marker
Small beakers or glass jars	

Planaria can be maintained in filtered pond water. Tap water that has aged by standing for several days to eliminate the chlorine is also suitable. Use a sharp razor blade or scalpel to cut a flatworm in half vertically and horizontally. This will separate the animal's head region from its tail region and its left side from its right side. Place each piece in a separate container with water. Be sure to label each container. Change the water daily, but do not feed regenerating *Planaria*. Keep them in a cool, dark place. Observe the progress each piece makes on a daily basis.

Next, cut a flatworm into thirds. What happens? Determine the smallest piece that can regenerate a new head or tail. If your cuts do not completely sever the animal, you can produce some interesting combinations. Occasionally, the separated pieces will rejoin and heal. If this happens, you will have to cut them again or keep them separated in some way.

Doing More

- Investigate the effects of ultraviolet light and chemicals such as colchicine, nicotine, and adrenalin on the rate of regeneration. Pass an electric current through the water as the *Planaria* regenerate. ***Caution: Ask an adult to help you check on safety factors before working with an electric current, especially one that passes through water.*** You can also explore the effect of an electromagnetic field on the rate of regeneration. If you discover something that has a significant effect, test its ability to influence the regenerative ability of an animal that cannot replace lost parts.

- One of the most active areas of human regeneration research focuses on spinal cord injuries. Some nerves, like those in the fingers, eventually grow back if they are damaged. However, nerves in the central nervous system—the brain and spinal cord—do not grow back after an injury. Even a minor break in the vertebrae that make up the spinal cord can result in permanent paralysis.

  Experimenting with humans to study regeneration is obviously out of the question, so scientists use goldfish and frogs for their studies on spinal cord regeneration. Hopefully, these animal models will provide some insight into ways of stimulating nerves in the human central nervous system so that they regenerate.

You can check out the latest in human spinal cord injury research on the Internet at *www.spinalcord.org/*. This site contains information on the use of electrical stimulation and tendon transfer surgery to restore hand function. You will also find links to other Internet resources. Checking this site may give you an idea for a project involving nerve regeneration in humans.

- Another active area of research on regeneration in humans has more to do with vanity than permanent disability. This area deals with male-pattern baldness. Some 35 million American men experience some degree of hair loss. Each year, they spend nearly $1 billion dollars on products in hopes of growing new hair. Hair is produced by follicle cells in the scalp. Once they die, these follicle cells cannot regenerate and can no longer produce hair.

  Two products, Rogaine and Propecia, have recently received much attention. Rogaine was recently approved as an over-the-counter drug, so you should have no trouble buying it at a local pharmacy. A recent study indicated that Propecia may inhibit the action of an enzyme known as 5-alpha-reductase. This enzyme appears to be present in higher levels in men with male-pattern baldness. Another study recently uncovered a *gene* responsible for a condition called alopecia universalis. This condition is characterized by the absence of eyebrows, eyelashes, body hair, and the gradual loss of hair on the top of the head. This gene was appropriately named the "hairless" gene. Scientists are currently searching for other genes that may lead to male-pattern baldness.

Search the library and the Internet for information on advances in treating male-pattern baldness. Key terms to use in your search include "male-pattern baldness," "Rogaine," "minoxidil," "Propecia," "finasteride," and "alopecia universalis." Your search may give you an idea for a project dealing with male-pattern baldness. In turn, your project may yield a finding that could have significant financial rewards.

GENETICS
AND
EVOLUTION

While shopping in a supermarket in the summer, you may have noticed small flies gathered near the fresh fruit. These flies have the scientific name *Drosophila melanogaster* and, for obvious reasons, are commonly known as fruit flies. Much of what we know about heredity—how traits are passed on from one generation to the next—comes from studying fruit flies.

Fruit flies are often used to study heredity, or genetics. Working with fruit flies is easy and requires little space. These flies are easy to maintain and breed. Large numbers can be kept in a small bottle with just a little food. Males and females mate readily. In addition, each female fly lays hundreds of eggs at a time, providing a new generation of flies every 2 weeks. Fruit flies have a number of inherited traits that are easy to observe and follow from one generation to the next.

Fruit flies are tiny insects. This photograph of
a fruit fly was taken through a microscope.

At the simplest level, a trait is controlled by two genes.
A gene can be defined as the basic unit of heredity. In
Chapter 6, you read about meiosis and learned that a
sperm and an egg each contribute half the chromosomes
found in a zygote. In organisms that use meiosis to reproduce, chromosomes come in pairs. One member of each
pair is obtained from the sperm, the other member from
the egg. Each chromosome pair may contain thousands of

genes. Scientists estimate that the 23 chromosome pairs in humans may contain as many as 100,000 genes. Fruit flies have four chromosomes.

STUDYING DOMINANCE

A gene for a particular trait is located at a specific site on a chromosome. For example, a gene that controls body color in *Drosophila* is located at a specific site on chromosome 2. Because chromosomes occur in pairs, genes also come in pairs. Each member of a gene pair is known as an *allele*. However, these two alleles may or may not be the same. If the two alleles for body color are the same, then the outcome is obvious. But what happens if the two alleles are different? For example, one allele may carry information for gray body color while the other allele carries information for black body color. Will the fruit fly have a black or gray body color? The answer depends on which trait is dominant.

A *dominant trait* masks, or dominates, the expression of the other trait in the pair. The trait that is masked is known as the *recessive trait*. In fruit flies, the allele for black body color is dominant, and the allele for gray body color is recessive. Thus, when one allele for black body color and one allele for gray body color are present, the fruit fly will have a black body.

Gregor Mendel, an Austrian monk who worked in the 1860s, was the first person to understand how this phenomenon works. Because he wondered how traits were passed on from one generation to the next, he studied heredity in garden peas. Mendel examined seven traits and observed that each trait had a dominant and a recessive form. Plant height, for example, could be either tall or short. Mendel found that tall was the dominant trait.

His experiments took many years to complete and required a lot of space. By using fruit flies, instead of pea plants, you can study dominance in a shorter time and in a smaller space.

WHICH TRAIT IS DOMINANT?

What You Need	
Drosophila melanogaster*	White index card
Ether	Tapered brush
Etherizer	Stereomicroscope
Vials containing food	Dropper
Cotton	Tape
Small glass jar	Petri dish
Cooking oil	

Obtain fruit flies with both forms of the trait you choose to study. For example, if you decide to determine whether red eye color or white eye color is dominant, you need to purchase flies with both eye colors. To carry out your project, you will have to learn how to etherize the flies.

Place several drops of ether in the etherizer. *Caution: Be careful when working with ether. It is flammable.* Gently tap the vial of flies to knock them to the bottom. Quickly remove the cotton plug from the vial and place it firmly over the etherizer. Tap the vial to transfer all the

---

* Scientific supply companies sell Drosophila. Because these companies often sell materials only to schools, ask your science teacher to place an order for you. You can buy flies with different eye colors, wing shapes, and body patterns.

flies into the etherizer. The ether will start to take effect in a few seconds.

Do not leave the flies in the etherizer for more than 1 minute. If you do, they will die. You can tell a fly is dead if its wings stick straight up from its body. Discard any dead flies in a small jar of cooking oil. Scientists generally refer to this as "the morgue."

Remove the bottom from the etherizer and pour the flies onto a white index card. Examine them under a stereomicroscope. Move the flies around with the brush. Be careful because they are easily injured. As you can see in Figure 11, females are easy to distinguish from males. The female has a larger body that ends in a point. The

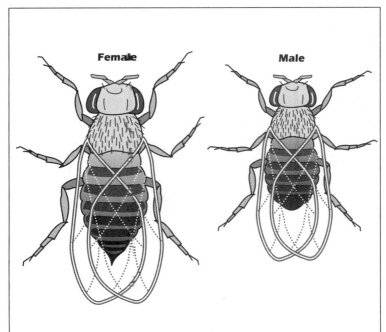

FIGURE 11 A female Drosophila is larger than a male. The female's body has a pointed end, while the male's body has a rounded end.

rear portion of the male's body is black, whereas the female has alternating dark and light bands extending to the end of her body.

The flies will start to wake up in about 5 minutes. You can etherize the flies again by covering them with a cotton wad taped to a petri dish cover. Just place a few drops of ether on the cotton before covering the flies. Be careful because flies are more easily killed by a second exposure to ether. When you have finished your examination, place the flies back in a vial and plug it with cotton. Set the vial on its side until all the flies have recovered from the ether. In this way, they will not become trapped and die in the food at the bottom.

If you want to save money, use baby-food jars instead of vials and make your own medium for maintaining *Drosophila*. Cook up a mixture of cornmeal, agar, molasses, and water. You will also have to add a small quantity of a preservative to prevent mold from developing in the medium. Fill the vial or jar about one-quarter full with the hot mixture. The liquid will solidify as the agar hardens. Some yeast sprinkled on the surface will serve as a food source. If the medium is too soft, the flies will get trapped in the food and die.

Now that you know how to work with fruit flies, start planning your project. For example, you can mate, or cross, flies with different wing lengths or different eye colors to determine which trait is dominant. You must use virgin females for all your crosses. This is the only way to be sure that the females are carrying unfertilized eggs and that only the traits you wish to study are involved in the cross.

To obtain virgin females, remove all the adult flies from a vial. New adults will emerge in about 10 hours. Virgin female flies emerge in the morning hours. Separate the newly emerged females immediately. Because the adult females have not mated, they can all be used for your crosses.

If you have decided to examine wing shape, place five virgin female flies with long wings in a vial with five males that have short or dumpy wings. Always perform the reciprocal cross: Place five virgin female flies with short wings and five male flies with long wings in another vial. Label all your vials with the date and the type of cross.

Store your vials at room temperature. Within a week, you should see the next generation hatching from the eggs. At this point, remove the parents so that you do not confuse them with their offspring, which will become adult flies in about 10 days. Etherize the new adults and observe them. What do you see? Continue your observations on the flies that emerge through day 17 of your experiment. The more first-generation flies included in your results, the better your chances of making an accurate conclusion. Do not return the flies to their original vials. Place them in new vials and use them to produce a new generation of flies. Compare your results to what Mendel observed with his second-generation pea plants. You can cross as many generations as you wish.

Doing More
- You may choose to do a project that studies two or more traits at the same time. For example, you can mate flies with normal wings and red eyes with flies lacking wings and having brownish-colored eyes. What do you think will happen? Ask your math teacher to help you do a statistical analysis of your results. Such a comparison often helps scientists realize that a trait is being inherited in an unusual way.

- Find out what happens when the flies' environment is changed. For instance, curly wings will develop only when flies are kept at 25°C. At room temperature, the wings will be straight. Examine other traits for sensitivity to temperature changes. Explore other environmental factors to see if a trait appears only under certain conditions. Experiment with various intensities of light, food additives, or changes in atmospheric pressure. If you notice a change, determine whether heredity is involved by using the fly in genetic crosses. Does the trait appear in future generations when the environment is changed and then disappear when original conditions are reestablished?

  Extend this project by examining humans to see whether various characteristics and behaviors are the result of heredity or environment. Scientists often refer to this as the study of nature versus nurture. The ideal subjects for this type of study are identical twins who were separated shortly after birth and raised in different homes. Identical twins have the same genetic makeup, so any differences in their behavior, attitudes, preferences, intelligence, and interests must be attributed to their environment. Obviously, identical twins are usually raised together, but scientists have found several sets who were not and have studied them. Check the library and search the Internet to learn what has been discovered in these studies.

- One environmental factor almost guaranteed to cause a trait to change is radiation. Any change in the genetic information is called a *mutation*. Exposing fruit flies to X rays has been used to produce mutations in wing patterns, eye colors, and other traits.

Contact a local hospital or university and ask to use their X-ray equipment to conduct a project on mutations. A technician must operate the equipment, but make sure to record the amount of radiation given to your flies. When you have identified an interesting mutation, use the fly in a genetic cross to study its pattern of inheritance.

Ultraviolet light and chemicals called mutagens can also cause mutations. Nitrous acid, DDT, formaldehyde, and mercury are all known mutagens. Some chemicals used as food additives, weed killers, and insecticides are suspected mutagens. Conduct a project using fruit flies to confirm a suspected mutagen or identify a new one. Check with a local research center or university to see whether someone there is studying the effects of mutagens. ***Caution: This type of project must be done under the close supervision of a scientist working in this area.***

- Scientists are concerned about the recent appearance of "superbugs"—bacteria that are resistant to antibiotics. If a "superbug" infects a person, the consequences can be fatal. Resistance to antibiotics is a genetic trait that bacteria can pass on. Drug companies are searching for new antibiotics that will prove effective in killing dangerous bacteria. You can approach this problem from a different angle. Can you design and carry out a project to alter the genetics of a resistant bacterial strain so that it can be killed by an antibiotic? You should work with a bacterial strain that poses no health hazard to humans. Check with a scientist working in this area for advice about the safety considerations.

DNA

Earlier in this chapter, a gene was defined as the basic unit of heredity. Actually, a gene can be defined in several different ways. Another definition is one that refers to a gene as a segment of DNA that directs the production of a particular protein. DNA is the chemical compound that stores an organism's hereditary information. The following project will show you how to extract DNA from peas.

EXTRACTING DNA

What You Need	
Protective eye goggles	Toothpicks
Rubbing alcohol	Clear liquid dishwashing detergent
Freezer	
Graduated cylinders	Refrigerator
Salt	Coffee filter
Warm water	Wire strainer
Peas	Plastic cup
Blender	Large plastic bowl with ice
Large plastic container	Meat tenderizer

Caution: Be sure to wear protective eye goggles while performing this procedure. Place the rubbing alcohol in the freezer. Next, dissolve 15 mL of salt in 355 mL of warm water. Place 118 mL of fresh peas in a blender, and cover the peas with the saltwater.* The salt contains positive charges that will neutralize the negative charges on the DNA you will extract. If the negative charges were not neutralized, they would repel one another and break down the DNA.

Blend the peas until they have the consistency of a thin soup. Transfer the pea soup to a plastic container. Gently stir in 118 mL of the dishwashing detergent. Mix the pea soup with a toothpick as you add the detergent. Stir and pour gently so as not to produce too many soap bubbles. The detergent will break down the membranes of the cell, releasing the DNA inside the nucleus. After all the detergent has been added, allow the mixture to stand for 5 minutes in a refrigerator. Keeping the mixture cool will prevent the DNA from breaking down.

After letting it stand for 5 minutes, pour the mixture through a coffee filter that has been placed in a wire strainer. Collect the filtrate (the liquid that passes through the filter) in a plastic cup that has been placed in a bowl of ice. Use the flat end of a toothpick to add one scoop of meat tenderizer to the filtrate. Stir the mixture with the toothpick. The meat tenderizer will break down any proteins present in the filtrate, leaving the DNA intact.

Slowly add an equal amount of ice-cold rubbing alcohol to the pea filtrate. Gently pour the alcohol so that it forms a layer on top of the filtrate. The DNA in the mixture will slowly rise from the filtrate and collect at the point where it meets the alcohol layer. The DNA should be clear and stringy. You can use a toothpick to spool the DNA. Simply swirl the toothpick as you would twist a

* If you are using dried or frozen peas, soak them in water for at least 30 minutes and drain off the water before putting the peas in the blender.

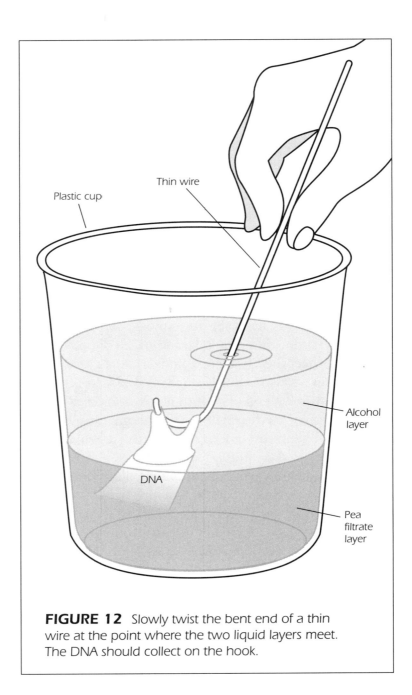

FIGURE 12 Slowly twist the bent end of a thin wire at the point where the two liquid layers meet. The DNA should collect on the hook.

fork to wrap spaghetti. If the DNA is too thick to remove with a toothpick, you can use a piece of thin wire with one end bent into the shape of a fishhook. See Figure 12. The DNA can be dried and frozen if you want to use it in additional experiments.

Use this same procedure to extract DNA from onions, liver, powdered yeast cells, and other sources. How does the DNA from different sources compare? Can one type be stretched farther than another? Which one is the thickest? Do they all respond the same way to treatment with various household chemicals, heat, and repeated freezing and thawing?

Doing More
Scientists are currently working to map the location of every gene on the human chromosomes. The Human Genome Project is an attempt to determine the sequence of the four basic chemical compounds that make up DNA. These compounds are adenine (A), thymine (T), guanine (G), and cytosine (C). The Human Genome Project has lasted many years and cost billions of dollars. Mapping a gene—determining its location on a chromosome—is not always such a difficult task. In fact, the genes on the chromosomes of fruit flies have been extensively mapped with relative ease.

A detailed chromosome map provides the order and position of each gene on a chromosome. Scientists need this information if they want to study a gene responsible for a disease or replace a defective gene with a functional one.

One method for mapping the location of genes involves working with giant chromosomes, such as those found in the salivary glands of *Drosophila*. The cells in these glands keep dividing without separating. Consequently, they are quite large and have distinctive light and

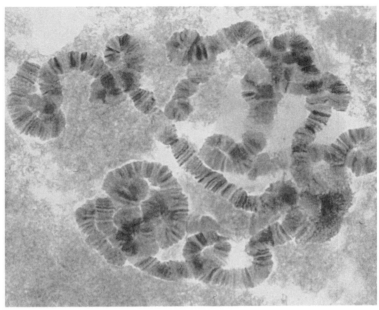

Fruit flies have giant chromosomes in their salivary glands. This photograph was taken through a microscope that magnified the image about 1,000 times.

dark bands. The salivary glands can be removed and stained to see the banding patterns. These bands can be used to look at particular genes.

For example, if a trait appears at the same time a band puffs up and becomes more distinct, the gene that causes the trait is probably located in the puffed-up area. If a chromosome has a flaw, such as a missing piece or an unusual shape, any observable change in the fruit fly could be linked to that area of the chromosome. As you can see, these giant chromosomes are an important tool for mapping genes. Human chromosomes, on the other hand, are small. To study their banding patterns, scientists grow human cells in culture where they are treated with chemicals to make the chromosomes swell. If the cells come from a person with a disease or an unusual trait, the bands can be compared to those in the chromosomes of a normal person. Any difference might pinpoint the location of the gene responsible for the disease or trait under study.

A rather sophisticated project could involve an attempt to culture cells from an animal or a plant with an unusual trait. Treat the cells with a chemical to enlarge the chromosomes. Then check the banding patterns. Compare them to those in the chromosomes of an organism lacking the unusual trait. Look for enlarged puffs, missing pieces, broken-off ends, or extra segments on one of the chromosomes. If something unusual is present, you have evidence linking the trait with a particular location on a chromosome.

EVOLUTION

Evolution is the process by which a group of organisms change over time. An individual organism cannot evolve, but populations of organisms—groups of males and females that mate and produce offspring—can and do evolve over generations.

One of the first scientists to study the evolution of populations was Charles Darwin, an English naturalist who began his work in the 1830s. Darwin recognized that if a population is provided with unlimited food, space, and resources and is protected from all predators, its size will increase at a phenomenal rate. For example, a single bacterial cell, dividing every 20 minutes, can produce 72 generations in just 24 hours! Obviously, this massive growth does not occur. In nature, the growth of a population is controlled by a number of factors, such as a limited food supply, presence of predators, disease, and lack of sufficient water. The following project will show you how populations actually grow.

OBSERVING POPULATION GROWTH

What You Need	
Packet of yeast	Test tube
Graduated cylinder	Medicine dropper
Warm water	Iodine
Glass jar	Ruled (2 × 2 mm) microscope slide
Balance	
Table sugar	Coverslips
1-mL pipettes	Compound microscope

Dissolve a packet of yeast in 80 mL of warm water in a glass jar. Add 20 g of sucrose (table sugar) and stir. Keep your yeast culture in a warm, dark area as you carry out your project.

Use a pipette to transfer 1 mL of the yeast culture to a test tube and add 2 drops of iodine. *Caution: Be careful not to get any iodine on your skin or in your eyes. It is a poison and an eye irritant.* The iodine will kill and stain the yeast cells, making them easier to observe. Use a 1-mL pipette to transfer 0.1 mL of the yeast-iodine mixture to the ruled microscope slide. After placing a coverslip on the slide, examine it under the low-power objective of a microscope.

Use the highest power to count the number of yeast cells in five 2 × 2 mm squares. Be sure to use a system when counting. For example, count the cells as you would read a page in a book. Start in the upper left-hand corner and proceed across the slide until you reach the end of the square. Then move the slide back to the left and continue counting. Record the number of yeast cells in the square. Repeat this process until you have counted the number of cells in five squares. Calculate the average number of yeast cells per square by dividing the total number by 5. To determine the number of yeast cells in 1 mL of culture, multiply the average number by 2,500. This number represents the number of yeast cells in the test tube.

Repeat the process of counting the number of yeast cells in 1 mL of culture every 24 hours. Stop counting when the number reaches a plateau. Graph your results, plotting the days on the x-axis and the number of yeast cells on the y-axis. Based on the shape of your graph, make as many conclusions as possible regarding the growth of the yeast population.

Investigate ways of affecting the growth pattern of a yeast population. You can vary the temperature, change the amount of sugar you add, increase the acidity of the growth media, or place a predator such as *Paramecia* in the culture.

Doing More

- *Drosophila* are also suitable for a project investigating the genetic advantage of certain organisms within a population. Genetic studies have indicated that individuals with two different alleles for a gene sometimes have an advantage in nature. Such individuals are said to be heterozygous for the trait. Those with two identical alleles for the trait are said to be homozygous. An individual may be either homozygous dominant or homozygous recessive.

Compare the number of offspring produced by heterozygous and homozygous individuals. With the help of your science teacher, obtain flies homozygous for a trait from a scientific supply company. If you mate flies homozygous for the dominant trait with flies homozygous for the recessive trait, then their offspring will be heterozygous. Mate these flies to see which type produces more offspring, especially under unfavorable conditions. If the heterozygous flies show superiority, manipulate their environment to reduce their reproductive advantage.

- Some interesting discoveries about evolutionary patterns have been made by examining small, isolated populations. Examples in human populations include the Amish in Pennsylvania and Hasidic Jews. People in both groups live in a tightly knit, isolated community. Individuals typically marry within the population. This close interbreeding has caused genes to be far from what is expected. In fact, an allele may even disappear within a small population. This is what happened to the northern elephant seal, *Mirounga angustirostris*. Check the library and search the Internet for information about these populations. Key terms to use include "genetic inbreeding" and "genetic drift." Your project can include both a report of this genetic phenomenon and a computer model that simulates how genetic drift operates.

- Darwin suggested that evolution operates on the basis of natural selection. In effect, the environment places a selection pressure on a population. Selection pressure means that organisms that are adapted to their environment can survive, reproduce, and pass their genes on to future generations. Those not adapted are more likely to die and thus less likely to pass on their genes. Given enough time, the organisms in the population might change or evolve.

Design a project to investigate the selection pressure exerted by the environment on different types of organisms within a population. Once again, *Drosophila* are suitable. Obtain flies with various wing patterns, eye colors, or body shapes. Place the same number of each type in identical vials. For example, put ten males and ten females with normal wings in one vial, put ten males and ten females with curly wings in a second vial, and so on. Count how many offspring are produced in each case. You could also take the larvae produced by various matings and place equal numbers in different vials. Record the number of adults that eventually hatch.

Experiment with changing the temperature, day-night cycle, and composition of the culture medium. Determine whether the same genetic type is favored in every situation. Repeat your studies by mixing two or three different types in the same vial. For example, place flies with normal wings with an equal number of flies with curly wings in the same vial. Record which type produces the most offspring or hatches most successfully. Again, manipulate the environment to see if one type shows a greater survival rate under different environmental conditions.

- One of the most active areas in biological research is genetic engineering. One of the outcomes of this research has been the tearing down of reproductive barriers between populations that had been established by evolution. For example, genes from humans are now routinely inserted into the chromosomes of other organisms, including bacteria. In addition, genetic engineering has made it conceivable that one day humans might control their own evolutionary future.

Some genetic-engineering researchers are searching for ways to correct inherited defects. For example, some people lack a gene that is needed for the immune system to function normally. Theoretically, inserting the gene into their DNA should cure this disease. Other researchers are working to improve the genetic makeup of entire populations of farm animals and crop plants. They hope to improve agricultural yields.

The possibilities for projects in this area are virtually unlimited. You can carry out a simple project with bacteria to show that genetic engineering can be done. Or you can try to design a method for inserting a gene into a person's DNA. To do this, you will have to work with a scientist engaged in this type of research. Such a project may be the start of your career as a scientist!

GLOSSARY

adenosine triphosphate (ATP)—an organic compound used for energy by a cell

allele—one member of a gene pair

amino acid—one of the organic compounds that are combined to build proteins

anaphase—the stage of mitosis in which members of each chromosome pair move toward opposite ends of a cell

callus—a mass of unspecialized cells that develops from a single cell

carbohydrate—an organic compound that serves as the body's principal energy source

cell membrane—the structure surrounding a cell, controlling what enters and leaves

chromosome—a structure inside the nucleus of a cell that contains a set of genes

clone—an organism that is produced from a single cell and is genetically identical to its parent

coacervate—a droplet formed by different kinds of organic compounds

contractile vacuole—a component of a cell that expels excess water

control group—in an experiment, a group that serves as a standard of comparison to another group that is identical in all respects but one

cotyledon—a tiny leaf that appears early in the development of a plant embryo *culture*—a procedure used to grow microorganisms, such as bacteria, in a controlled environment

deoxyribonucleic acid (DNA)—the chemical compound that stores the genetic information of an organism

dependent variable—the factor in an experiment that depends on how the independent variable is manipulated

diffusion—the movement of a substance from an area of high concentration to an area of lower concentration

dominant trait—a trait that masks, or dominates, another trait resulting from the same gene

embryo—a fertilized egg cell that has started to develop

enzyme—a compound, usually a protein, that speeds up the rate of a chemical reaction

eukaryote—a cell that contains a nucleus and other internal structures

evolution—the process by which a population changes over generations

experimental group—in an experiment, a group that is subjected to the factor being tested

extracellular digestion—the breakdown of food materials outside a cell

gene—the basic unit of heredity; composed of DNA

genetics—the study of heredity

germination growth and development of a seed

heredity—the transmission of traits from one generation to the next

independent variable—the factor that an experimenter is free to manipulate

infusion culture—a procedure used to obtain a large number of microorganisms by mixing water and a source, such as hay or wheat, where microorganisms are likely to be found

inorganic compound—a material that, with few exceptions, lacks carbon

intracellular digestion—the breakdown of food materials within the interior of a cell

lipid—an organic compound that includes fats

meiosis—the division of a sex cell that produces cells with half the original chromosome number

metaphase—the stage of mitosis in which chromosome pairs align themselves along the equator of a cell

microorganism—an organism that can be seen only with the use of magnification (microscope)

microsphere—a droplet of liquid surrounded by a protein membrane

mitosis—the process by which a cell divides to produce two genetically identical cells

multicellular—composed of many cells

mutation—a change in the genetic material of an individual

mycorrhizae—(pl. *mycorrhizae*) the mutual relationship between fungi and plant roots

negative feedback—a process in which a change in one direction eventually causes the system to change in the opposite direction

nucleus—the part of a cell that directs most of its activities

organ—a body part; a collection of tissues that function as a unit

organic compound—a material that contains carbon and hydrogen

osmoregulation—the ability of an organism to maintain a nearly constant internal water concentration despite changes in its environment

osmosis—the diffusion of water through a membrane

prokaryote—a cell that lacks a nucleus and other internal structures

prophase—the stage of mitosis in which the chromosomes shorten and become visible

protein—an organic compound that is made from amino acids

recessive trait—a trait that is masked, or dominated, by another trait resulting from the same gene

system—a group of organs that carry out a common function

telophase—the stage of mitosis in which the original cell begins to divide to form two cells

tissue—group of cells specialized to form a particular function

wet mount—a specimen prepared for microscopic observation by placing it in a small amount of liquid and adding a coverslip

zygote—a fertilized egg cell

RESOURCES

BOOKS

Bleifeld, Maurice. *Experimenting with a Microscope*, New York, NY: Franklin Watts, 1988.

Dykstra, Mary. *The Amateur Zoologist*, New York, NY: Franklin Watts, 1994.

Gardner, Robert. *Science Project Ideas About Trees*, Springfield, NJ: Enslow Publishers, 1997.

Gardner, Robert and David Webster. *Science Project Ideas About Animal Behavior*, Springfield, NJ: Enslow Publishers, 1997.

Gardner, Robert and Richard Adams. *Ideas for Science Projects*. Danbury, CT: Franklin Watts, 1997.

Tocci, Salvatore. *How to Do a Science Fair Project*, Danbury, CT: Franklin Watts, 1997.

VanCleave, Janice. *Biology for Every Kid: One Hundred & One Easy Experiments that Really Work*, New York , NY: John Wiley & Sons, Inc., 1990

Wells, Marion. *Biology Investigations*, Dubuque, IA: Kendall-Hunt Publishing Co., 1995

INTERNET SITES

Access Excellence
http://www.accessexcellence.org/
Take a look at the "What's News" (science updates), "Let's Collaborate"(online projects), and "Activities Exchange" (activities-to-go) sections.

Hands On Science Outreach
http://www.hands-on-science.org/
One section of this site is devoted to young scientists. It has information on projects to do at home and an opportunity to get feedback.

Information Unlimited
http://www.amazing1.com
This company sells plans for constructing a variety of items, including those needed to grow bacteria and fungi at home.

SciCentral
http://scicentral.com.
This science and engineering megadirectory is maintained by professional scientists. The K–12 Science page includes a Science Fair Project Resource Guide. Another section is entitled "Today's Research Highlights."

SCIENCE SUPPLY COMPANIES
Many science supply companies sell their merchandise only to schools—not to individuals. If you need chemicals or equipment that are not readily available, your science teacher may let you borrow them from the school. If not, ask your teacher for a catalog from one of the following companies. By looking through the catalog, you may be able to think of a way to substitute available materials for scientific equipment. Coming up with these types of substitutes shows ingenuity and will impress anyone who takes the time to look at your project. If there seems to be no substitute, ask your teacher to order the equipment for you.

Carolina Biological Supply Company
2700 York Road
Burlington, NC 27215-3398
http://www.carolina.com/

Connecticut Valley Biological Supply
PO Box 326
Southampton, MA 01073

Edmund Scientific
101 E. Gloucester Pike
Barrington, NJ 08007
http://www.edsci.com/
This company will mail any item they carry directly to your home. They have a variety of items that can be valuable for carrying out a biology project. Write them for a copy of their catalog.

WARD's Natural Science Establishment Inc.
P.O. Box 92912
Rochester, NY 14692-9012
http://www.wardsci.com/

INDEX

ABOUT THE AUTHOR

Salvatore Tocci taught chemistry and biology at East Hampton High School on Long Island, New York, for many years. His strong belief that science is best learned when students are actively involved has led him to write many science project books for high school students. In addition, Mr. Tocci has organized science fairs at his high school and judged both regional and national contests. He has also presented workshops for science teachers at meetings held throughout the United States. Mr. Tocci has published extensively and is the senior author of a high school text book that focuses on the practical applications of chemistry.